PRAISE FOR CANCELING *CAN'T*

"Some of the most meaningful, helpful, life-changing conversations I have ever had usually happened in a booth in some diner, with fellow Christians and a good cup of coffee. This is what I love about Mark and Joe's book, *Canceling Can't*. The format and style are so engaging. It is as if you are sitting at a table with the authors, taking in the wisdom, and walking away better off for it. *Canceling Can't* is maybe the most practical and helpful book you will ever read. It is a reservoir of accumulated wisdom, straight from the heart of Joe and Mark, reflecting a combined eighty-plus years in ministry and grounded firmly in the Bible.

"*Canceling Can't* is a call to victorious living. As children of God, we need not live defeated lives. We serve a can-do God who can do more than we ever think or imagine! (Eph 3:20). This book provides hope and practical, biblical help for those who may find themselves currently in a pit of despair and defeat. It also provides great insights, stories and illustrations for those who want to help others get out."

—**Al Serhal**
Executive Director, Hippo Valley Christian Mission

"As a seven-time iron distance triathlon finisher, the word *can't* is not in my vocabulary. At least as it relates to physical accomplishments. Spiritually? Well, that's another question. Mark Atteberry and Joe Putting have hit a home run with *Canceling Can't!* Their many decades of ministry experience are woven throughout this book in a way that will inspire you to realize that getting rid of the negative *can'ts* and focusing on what God can do in and through you will transform every aspect of your life. You want to experience positive change? You want to see your relationship with God and others in a whole new light? Read it! Share it! Live it!"

—**Travis Jacob**
Executive Director of Advance Center for Ministry Training, author of *Ultimate Synergy: Building and Maintaining a Winning Culture in Your Organization*

"I have a basic rule: if Mark Atteberry writes it, I'm buying it and reading it. From *The Samson Syndrome* to *The Ten Dumbest Things Christians Do* to *The Solomon Seduction* to *Someone Knows*—one of the best novels I've ever read. I got 'em all and read 'em all and encouraged friends to do the same. His latest, along with dynamic pastor Joe Putting, which you now hold in your hands, deals with eight issues we all face, and does so powerfully and practically. All while making you smile, laugh, and occasionally say, 'ouch!' You're gonna love this book, and here's my prediction: you can't put it down!"

—**Barry L. Cameron**
Pastor for fifty-plus years and bestselling author of
The ABCs of Financial Freedom

"If you think you can't, think again. Those of us who worry about the future, wrestle with insecurity, struggle with doing what we know is right, and feel hopeless more often than we care to admit can take heart. Mark Atteberry and Joe Putting are here to help. In *Canceling Can't*, they share their wisdom—acquired through decades of ministry experience—in a way that will lift your spirit and restore your confidence. Yes, my friend, you *can*!"

—**Mike Kocolowski**
Chief Stewardship Officer of Christian Financial Resources and author of *Happily Generous: The Secret to Living a Priceless Life*

"*Canceling Can't* is a powerful book that will help you reclaim what so many of us have lost. Mark Atteberry and Joe Putting dismantle the barriers and limiting beliefs we often accept as unchangeable while offering a new mindset with new possibilities. With brave audacity this book will have you removing the word *can't* from your vocabulary and replacing it with *can*. A must-read for anyone ready to break free from self-imposed limits and embraces new opportunities.

—**Crockett Davidson**
Executive Pastor, Lifepointe Church

Canceling Can't

Eliminating the Word
— and Attitude —
That's Stealing Your Joy
and Wrecking Your Life

MARK ATTEBERRY &
JOE PUTTING

Canceling *Can't*

Copyright © 2024 by Mark Atteberry and Joe Putting

All rights reserved. No part of this book may be reproduced in any form or by any means—whether electronic, digital, mechanical, or otherwise—without permission in writing from the publisher, except by a reviewer, who may quote brief passages in a review.

Unless otherwise noted, all Scripture from the *Holy Bible*, New Living Translation, copyright © 1996, 2004, 2015 by Tyndale House Foundation. Used by permission of Tyndale House Publishers, Inc., Carol Stream, Illinois 60188. All rights reserved. Scripture marked ESV is taken from The Holy Bible, English Standard Version. ESV® Text Edition: 2016. Copyright © 2001 by Crossway Bibles, a publishing ministry of Good News Publishers. Scripture marked HCSB is taken from the Holman Christian Standard Bible (HCSB) copyright © 1999, 2000, 2002, 2003, 2009 by Holman Bible Publishers, Nashville Tennessee. All rights reserved. Scripture marked NIV is taken from the Holy Bible, New International Version®, NIV® Copyright ©1973, 1978, 1984, 2011 by Biblica, Inc.® Used by permission. All rights reserved worldwide.

The views and opinions expressed in this book are those of the authors and do not necessarily reflect the official policy or position of Illumify Media Global.

Published by
Illumify Media Global
www.IllumifyMedia.com
"Let's bring your book to life!"

Paperback ISBN: 978-1-964251-24-0

Cover design by Debbie Lewis

Printed in the United States of America

Joe Putting

To my dad, Robert Putting. He went to be with the Lord at the age of eighty-nine. I've never met a more selfless man. Dad had to drop out of high school to help with the farm and later got his GED. He retired from a career at McDonald Douglas Corporation. This man was married for sixty-three years and has three children, two with a master's degree and one with a doctorate! Not many men like that anymore. Thanks Pop!

Mark Atteberry

To the wonderful people who make up the First Christian Church of Frostproof, Florida. After forty-six years of preaching and four years of retirement, I thought I was done in the pulpit. Then one day my phone rang, and I was back in the saddle. And the saddle has never felt so good. Thank you, FCCF for helping to put the icing on my ministry cake.

Contents

Foreword xi
Introduction xiii

1 Yes, You *Can* Get Out of That Pit 1
2 Yes, You *Can* Find Justice in an
   Unjust World 25
3 Yes, You *Can* Feel Good About Your Future
   in a Deteriorating World 46
4 Yes, You *Can* Live Courageously in a
   Terrifying World 69
5 Yes, You *Can* Conquer Your
   Besetting Sin 92
6 Yes, You *Can* Live Righteously in
   a Cesspool 114
7 Yes, You *Can* Live Guilt-Free with a Long
   Rap Sheet 134
8 Yes, You *Can* Find the "Perfect" Church ... 154

Questions for Quiet Reflection or
   Group Discussion 179
About the Authors 188

Foreword

IN A WORLD WHERE voices of defeat and despair often drown out the whispers of hope and possibility, co-authors Pastor Joe Putting and Mark Atteberrry bring us a timely and profound message in their book, *Canceling Can't*. With clarity and conviction, they delve into the heart of a pervasive lie propagated by the enemy—that we are bound by our weaknesses and incapable of change. Through a faithful exploration of Scripture, they unveil the truth that through the power of the Holy Spirit and the truth of God's Word we can break free from the chains of immorality, inadequacy, injustice and more.

Drawing from a wealth of biblical passages, Joe and Mark illuminate a path toward moral living, abundance, and justice. They dismantle the myths that imprison our hearts and minds, replacing them with the liberating truth that God has equipped us with everything we need to live victoriously. Each chapter is a beacon of hope, guiding us through the transformative power of God's Word and Spirit, inviting us to embrace a life of purpose, integrity, and compassion.

As you embark on this journey through *Canceling Can't*, prepare to be challenged and encouraged. This book is not merely a theological exploration but a practical guide for those seeking to reclaim their identity and destiny in Christ. It is a call to arms against the forces of darkness that seek to rob us of our potential. Through insightful exposition and heartfelt exhortation, you will discover that with God nothing is impossible and every promise is within reach.

May this book be a source of inspiration and empowerment, reminding us all that in Christ we are more than conquerors.

—**Cord Bear**
Executive Pastor
Tomoka Christian Church

Introduction

A Declaration of War

*I can do everything through Christ,
who gives me strength.*
Philippians 4:13

THIS BOOK IS A declaration of war against a word we believe has done more damage to people than any other: the word *can't*.

As of this writing, we have spent a combined eighty-four years in local church ministry, which means we have worked with thousands of troubled people who came to us for help. We've spent many thousands of hours listening to them tell their stories and pour out their hearts. We've prayed and wept with them. We've walked with them through their struggles, sometimes for months and years. And the thing we've noticed is that virtually all of them come to us in the beginning using this enslaving, defeating, spirit-crushing, life-destroying word:

"I can't forgive her after what she did."

"I know he's married, but I can't quit thinking about him."

"I'm getting an abortion because I can't take care of this baby."

"I can't be happy living as a man when I know I'm really a woman."

"My wife and I just can't get along. The only answer for us is divorce."

"I know what the Bible says about homosexuality, but I can't help how I feel."

Can't.

Can't.

Can't.

Can't.

Every God-defying excuse, every Scripture-violating rationalization, every life-destroying evasion of truth we've ever heard has had the word *can't* in it. It's the common denominator in the stories of all the people we've met who were living in misery, suffering in shame, and feeling hopeless. We're talking about people from all walks of life: male and female, married and single, rich and poor. All colors, all levels of education, and all political persuasions. The word *can't* is an equal opportunity wrecking ball, which is why we're convinced it's one of Satan's favorite words, if not his very favorite.

Oddly, the word *can't* does have a good side. It's a very helpful word when used to set parameters and define truth. For example, Jesus said, "You can't serve two masters" (Matthew 6:24). He also said, "You can't come to the Father except through me" (John 14:6) and "Unless you are born again you can't see the Kingdom of God" (John 3:3). It is no exaggeration to say that our salvation depends on this word that so beautifully clarifies God's will and debunks false doctrines.

INTRODUCTION

It's also a great word for parents: "You can't go play until you clean up your room."

A great word for coaches: "You can't be a champion if you don't give max effort."

A great word for doctors: "You can't keep up this pace if you want to stay healthy."

A great word for teachers: You can't get a scholarship without good grades."

But for every one time we've heard *can't* used in a helpful way, we've heard it used in a destructive way hundreds, perhaps thousands, of times. It's the destructive aspect of this word that we are declaring war on.

As we see it, Satan has employed two key strategies that have helped him turn this word into one of his most lethal weapons.

Strategy #1: Convince people that can't is a liberating word.

To struggling married couples he whispers, "If you just can't get along, then get divorced and move on with your life. You've beaten your head against the wall long enough. You deserve to be free from this."

To women who are inconveniently pregnant he whispers, "If you can't give this baby the attention it needs, then it's better to get an abortion. You don't want to be saddled with a kid while you're chasing your dream. You need to be free to do whatever it takes to succeed."

To the gender dysphoric he says, "If you can't stand hiding your true self, then come out and be who you really are. Only then will you be free to find true happiness."

See how it works? Satan will try to convince you that God's path is closed to you—that you *can't* go God's way—and then show you an alternative path and claim it's the only way to find freedom and relief from your terrible situation. Sadly, it won't be until you're well down that path to "freedom" that you start seeing the dead bodies of those who believed the lie before you. Solomon warned us of this when he wrote of the way that seems right to man but ends in destruction (Proverbs 14:12). The only reason Satan's deadly, alternative path seems right to us is because we believe his can'ts.

Strategy #2: Convince people that can't is a fact-based word.

"It's a fact. You two can't get along."

"It's a fact. You can't take care of this baby."

"It's a fact. You can't be happy living in denial of your true gender identity."

Satan wants us to accept his can'ts as fact, and we often do so because it feels good in the moment. It gives us a sense of relief. It allows us to feel good about what he's encouraging us to do. Never mind that there's a mountain of evidence that exposes Satan's so-called facts as lies:

INTRODUCTION

All the troubled couples who saved their marriages.

All the women who kept their babies and were glad they did.

All the people who had nothing but regret after transitioning.

We are convinced that God filled the Bible with stories of miracles to constantly remind us that all things really *are* possible with him (Matthew 19:26) and that, far from being fact based, Satan's can'ts are always feelings based. When he comes whispering in our ears, he's *always* playing on our feelings.

Another important fact that has fueled our desire to write this book is what the word *can't* does to our relationship with God. Remember when God called Moses out of a burning bush to go to Egypt to confront Pharaoh and demand the release of God's people, the Israelites, from slavery? Immediately, Moses went into his "I can't" routine. He pointed out that he was a nobody who lacked the gravitas needed to stand before a head of state (Exodus 3:11). Then he claimed he wasn't an articulate speaker and would make a mess of things (Exodus 4:10). God graciously put up with his excuses at first, but not for long. Exodus 4:14 says, "Then the Lord became angry with Moses."

For an even more striking example, think about the Israelites' reaction when they arrived at the Jordan River. God had led them there, promising to give them the land of Canaan which was just on the other side of the water. But when the spies returned with a report about giants in the land, the people said, "Whoa, hang on. They're too powerful. We can't defeat them!" To say God was displeased would be the biggest understatement of all time. As punishment, he sent them into the wilderness to live until every single person who used the word *can't* dropped dead (Numbers 14:29).

It is no coincidence that every person we've heard use the word *can't* as an excuse or justification for questionable choices had a strained or broken relationship with God. And why wouldn't they? The "can't" mindset is anti-God through and through. It's a repudiation of his will, his promises, and most of all, his power. People who cling to this word will never, ever have a healthy relationship with him.

For all of these reasons, we are declaring war on the word *can't*. It's ruined enough lives, broken enough families, destroyed enough dreams, built enough walls between people and God. It may be doing all of these things to you right now. Is there something you need to do, need to change, need to fix that Satan has convinced you can't be done?

In the coming pages you'll find eight chapters, each one dealing with a different situation that has become a prison for millions of people. We're going to expose the can't-based lies on which those prisons are built, and show you how to break down the walls and move forward in freedom and victory. We're not promising that the paths forward from these situations will be easy. In fact, we'll tell you right now that they'll be hard—maybe harder than anything you've ever attempted. But we make no apology for that, just as

INTRODUCTION

Jesus made no apology when he talked about cutting off hands and plucking out eyeballs to overcome sin (Matthew 5:27–30). As we said right out of the gate: this is war. The goal here is not to fool around with half-measures or play little word games so you can feel better about your imprisonment. That's the world's way. Our goal is to help you fight the tough battles and find total freedom and victory in Christ.

Yes, in Christ.

This is not going to be a rah-rah session like you might experience at a sales rally where some hyper-enthusiastic motivational speaker with perfect hair is throwing out success principles and pushing you to climb to the next level. That's not us. We believe that freedom from every form of bondage, every plot of Satan, every enslaving habit, and every insidious lie is found in Christ. Paul the apostle said, "I can do everything through Christ, who gives me strength" (Philippians 4:13). This is why we're not going to be giving you a lot of our personal opinions. Experiences and stories that attest to the truthfulness of God's word, yes, but when it comes to the part about what it takes to be free, we're going to let the Scriptures speak.

We want you to someday be able to make that same statement Paul made, to give an impactful testimony of the power of Christ, and to hold up the story of your liberation from Satan's can'ts as exhibit A to prove your case. We want you to be able to say to others what we're saying to you: Through Christ, you *can*!

If that's what you want too, if you're tired of being imprisoned and ready to start living God's cans instead of Satan's can'ts, turn the page and keep reading.

1

YES, YOU *CAN* GET OUT OF THAT PIT

*You will restore me to life again and lift me up
from the depths of the earth.*
Psalm 71:20

IN OCTOBER OF 2022, a group of five tourists at the Grand Canyon Caverns in Arizona rode an elevator twenty-one stories underground to see some of the largest dry caverns in the country. When they were ready to return topside, they filed into the elevator and watched as the attendant pushed the UP button.

Nothing happened.

The attendant pushed the button a second time.

Nothing happened again.

At this point, the tourists were glancing nervously at each other. *They're messing with us. This is probably part of the routine. Throw a little scare into the tourists and then have a good laugh and ride the elevator to the top with everybody chuckling.*

Except it wasn't part of the routine. It wasn't a joke. The elevator was broken, for real.

If you've been to the Grand Canyon Caverns, you know that there is a system of stairs—twenty-one flights to be exact—that people could climb in the case of an elevator failure. The problem that day was that a couple of elderly people who were physically unable to make the climb were on this particular tour. As a show of solidarity, the tourists who could climb out decided to stay with the ones who couldn't.

Topside, officials were scrambling, trying to figure out what to do. They finally decided on a rope rescue operation. Each of the tourists was placed in a harness and raised by rope up the elevator shaft. Once they got set up, it took about fifteen minutes per person to lift the tourists out of the shaft. Each of the tourists was checked out medically when they reached the top and determined to have suffered no medical issues as a result of the experience.

There is, however, one not-so-small detail we omitted from this story. It caused our eyes to pop open when we read it.

At the bottom of the elevator shaft at the Grand Canyon Caverns there is a hotel suite.

A hotel suite?

Yes, a hotel suite.

If the rope rescue had been impossible for any reason, the tourists could have simply stayed in the hotel suite until the elevator was fixed.

This has become our prayer: *Father in heaven, if your will ever calls for either of us to be stranded in a deep hole in the ground, could you please make it one with a hotel suite?*

Unfortunately, most holes in the ground don't come so equipped. Rather, they are dark and musty and claustrophobic. And psychologically damaging, which is why terrorists often throw their kidnap victims into empty wells. I (Mark) read about one kidnap victim that was thrown into a well with water up to his knees. Every couple of hours, his kidnappers would lift the lid off the well and toss in a large snake. It was their way of breaking their captive and bending him to their will. He would agree to anything to get out of that well.

In Psalm 71, the psalmist (whom many people believe was David) speaks of his belief that God would raise him up "from the depths of the earth" (v. 20). Some have suggested that this is a messianic prophecy concerning the resurrection, but the more common interpretation is that David was simply referring to God's ability to rescue people from pits, or from seemingly hopeless situations.

Here are some facts about pits that we have noticed.

First, some of them are part of the natural landscape. The Grand Canyon Caverns, for example, weren't made by hard-hatted laborers with picks and shovels. Nobody got up one day and said, "Let's go make some caverns!" Likewise, some of the metaphorical pits that people find themselves in are not made with human hands. For example, when your closest loved one dies unexpectedly of a heart attack or stroke and leaves you alone and desperately lonely, there's no one to blame. It's just one of those things that happen occasionally in a fallen world.

Second, some pits are man-made. If you've ever been a scam victim, you know this to be true. One man we read about fell in love with a female soldier who was serving in Afghanistan. Through pictures and emails, they became very close. When she claimed to need money, he sent it, not once, but several times. They even set a wedding date, but she had to keep moving it back because of changes in her deployment orders. Meanwhile, she kept needing money and he kept sending it. Twenty thousand dollars later, after the man's life savings was depleted, it became apparent that the woman didn't exist.

It's good for us to remember that every moment of every day, evil people are digging pits in which they hope to trap the unsuspecting. The prophet Jeremiah said, "Among my people are wicked men who lie in wait for victims like a hunter hiding in a blind. They continually set traps to catch people" (Jeremiah 5:26). Our recommendation is to be suspicious of everything.

Finally, some pits are self-made. At the beginning of this book, we referenced the thousands of troubled people we have worked with in our combined eighty-four years in ministry. Many of those names and faces we have long forgotten, but what we haven't forgotten is the similarity of their stories: *I did [fill in bad choice]. I know I shouldn't have done it, but I was [fill in excuse]. Now I'm in a real mess (pit), and I don't know what to do (how to get out). Can you help me?*

The Bible talks about us falling into pits we dig ourselves (Psalm 7:15). We've seen it over and over again. People are disobedient at worst and reckless at best. They make bad decisions that often lead to worse decisions. Have you noticed this? Very few people stop at one bad decision. Our bad decisions often compound as we push the envelope further and further, or else try to cover up our nefarious doings instead of just humbling ourselves and repenting like the Bible says we should. It's the perfect metaphor for digging a pit, shovelful after shovelful, bad decision after bad decision. The first bad decision is like a shovelful of dirt tossed aside at our feet. Before long, we're tossing shovelfuls over our shoulder and then over our head as the pit grows deeper and deeper.

In the countless counseling sessions we've done, again and again we have looked the counselee in the eye and said, "You are your own worst enemy." We have never said this with anything but the utmost concern and compassion. We hate to see people suffer. But we also refuse to lie to people. They generally want to blame someone or something else for their problems when they are actually at fault, either because of something they did or, in some cases, something they failed to do.

If you're in one of these metaphorical pits, if you feel stuck or stranded in a hard place and have no idea how to get out, the first thing you need to do is think about how you got in there in the first place.

Canceling Can't

I (Mark) once talked to a woman who was unhappily married and looking for answers. What made her somewhat unique is that she was on her fifth husband. She was like a baseball player who had struck out four times and was now standing in the batter's box for the fifth time—and with two strikes! I said to her, "So why do you think you've had such bad experiences in marriage?" She immediately launched into a diatribe about what was wrong with each of her husbands, why they were impossible to get along with, and why she had to get out of those marriages to save her sanity. As kindly as possible, I said, "I hear you. But you know, if a baseball player strikes out four times, he will look at video, not of the pitcher, but of his swing. The first thing he will want to know is what *he* is doing wrong." Then I asked her if she felt she bore any responsibility for the marital troubles she'd had. She claimed that she was not perfect, but that she was definitely not the problem in her marriages. My hunch was that she was much more responsible than she was willing to admit to herself. If nothing else, she was lousy at choosing husbands.

If you're in a pit, you must be brutally honest with yourself. We know it's easy to make excuses. We've done it ourselves. But excuses are the single biggest thing that will keep you trapped in your pit if it is indeed one you dug yourself.

How to Be Honest with Yourself

Since honest self-evaluation is hard for everyone, we'd like to offer some hard-earned advice that will help you do it. Here are three "mirrors" you can look into that will show you your true self.

Mirror #1: Your Relationships

I (Joe) am an expert on this one. People who know me will tell you that I never lack for an opinion and know exactly what I would like to see happen at any given time. This is not necessarily a bad thing, but it can cause me to try too hard to bend the church I serve to *my* will instead of allowing God to lead us where *he* wants us to go. When I fall into this trap, the people around me suffer. My elders, my staff, my wife, and my kids find me pushy, demanding, and irritable, which creates tension on all sides. I can remember feeling completely frustrated the first time this happened. I couldn't figure out why I seemed to be at odds with everybody around me. If not for a kind soul who was honest with me, I don't know if I would have figured out that they weren't the problem, I was. I still remember going out and sitting on a picnic table and crying and promising God that I would give him back his church.

It's not just true for me; it's true for all of us. When something is amiss in our own hearts, it impacts our relationships. In fact, I'll go so far as to say this: When multiple people in your life are frustrated with you—especially those who are close to you and love you—that is the reddest of red flags. You can be pretty sure that something in your heart or mind needs to be corrected.

Mirror #2: Your Metrics

In 2023, Bud Light hired transgender activist Dylan Mulvaney, a biological male who believes he is a woman, to advertise their beer. Several commercials were made that showed Mr. Mulvaney prancing around in a dress and acting not like a woman but an immature adolescent female. The ads were so offensive to people that Bud Light's sales didn't just decline, they crashed. The company lost five billion dollars of its value in just a few months because people refused to buy their product. Those are some bad metrics.

Metrics are the numbers that tell the story, and they are everywhere all the time: blood pressure, temperature, prices reductions, price increases, sales receipts, gas mileage, interest rates, inflation, attendance figures, miles per hour, weight loss, weight gain, the list goes on and on. Even your day-to-day decisions create metrics.

We've counseled troubled people who used to go to church every Sunday, but tapered off to almost nothing, or dropped out altogether. That's a metric that speaks volumes.

We've also counseled people who once gave generously to the Lord's work but over time slowed and even stopped their giving. Another telling metric.

We've counseled people who had multiple marriages, an inordinate number of jobs that didn't work out, gigantic credit card balances, multiple foreclosures, multiple speeding tickets, and on and on. It's true that one concerning metric by itself doesn't necessarily mean a lot, but when you have several, that's a pretty clear indication that your life is not tracking in a healthy—let alone godly—direction.

What kind of metrics are you producing?

The NFL Hall of Fame coach Bill Parcells is credited with saying, "You are what your record says you are." Translated: You are what your metrics say you are.

Mirror #3: Your Bible

This is the most important mirror of them all. Like all preachers, we have long been frustrated by the large number of Christians who don't read the Bible. Many make the excuse that they can't understand it. But we think the greater likelihood is something along the lines of what Mark Twain said: "It's not the parts of the Bible I don't understand that bother me; it's the parts I do understand."

Have you ever bought a large piece of furniture, or maybe a gas grill, that had to be assembled? You open the box and there are pieces and panels and screws of all sizes and washers and dowel rods and who knows what else. You lay everything out on the floor, and then the first thing you do is call yourself an idiot for not paying the extra money to have the thing assembled. The second thing you do is find the directions. Those directions are the only hope you have of still being a sane person in two hours—and of having a piece of furniture that actually looks like what you bought. Seems like a no-brainer, right? Yet countless people think they can assemble the piece just fine without the directions.

One of the primary dangers of not following directions is having to take the piece of furniture apart and start over when you realize you missed a crucial step. This is a metaphor for the way many people live their lives. They think they can ignore God's directions, and everything will be just fine. Then when they make a mess of things, they come to people like us for help. What do we do? Pull out the directions (the Bible) and show them what they should have done (and could have done) from the beginning.

The Bible is the ultimate truth-teller. Your friends (or even your preacher) will try to say things in ways that don't crush your feelings, but the Bible just says it straight out with no sugarcoating. And you know what? That's what pit dwellers need! You don't get out of a pit by being mollycoddled and told your pit experience could happen to anybody, or that you are a victim. On the contrary, that's precisely the kind of thinking that keeps people in their pits for years.

How to Get Out of Your Pit

Once you've faced up to your pit reality and the reasons why you're in there, it's time to start the process of getting out. Here are three things you must do.

Believe you're not alone in your pit.

One of our favorite Bible stories is found in Daniel 3. Nebuchadnezzar, the king of Babylon, a man whose greatest attribute was not humility, commissioned the creation of a ninety-foot-tall gold statue of himself. He then issued an edict that whenever anyone heard the sound of music, they must bow to the ground and worship the statue. If they didn't, they would be thrown into a blazing furnace.

Since most people prefer living to dying, compliance with an edict like this is generally a given. But in this case, three young Hebrew men—Shadrach, Meshach, and Abednego—who'd earned respect and been given oversight responsibilities in the province, said, "Nope. We're not doing it. We'll bow to the one true God and no one else."

Naturally, they were reported. And naturally, Nebuchadnezzar had a meltdown. He simply couldn't have people openly defying him. The *How to Be King Handbook* covers this on page one: "You've got to show people who's boss." And so he did. He had our three heroes thrown right into the fire.

Then comes the best part of the story.

Shadrach, Meshach, and Abednego didn't lose their cool in the fire. Literally. Even when it was stoked seven times hotter than usual, they never broke a sweat and their clothes weren't singed, even though the guys who had to get close enough just to throw them in were burnt to a crisp. And if that wasn't mind-blowing enough, there actually appeared to be a fourth man in the fire. Someone the king and his cohorts thought looked like a god (Daniel 3:25).

The end of the story is that the boys didn't burn, and their clothes didn't even smell like smoke. Nebuchadnezzar attributed their survival to their God and issued a decree that anyone in the kingdom who spoke a word against the God of Shadrach, Meshach, and Abednego would be torn limb from limb (Daniel 3:29). (The man was big on horrifyingly brutal punishments.)

The question for us is, who was the fourth man in the fire? Smart people have debated this for centuries. Some think it was preincarnate Jesus while others think it was an angel. We're inclined to go with the Jesus crowd, but here's the important thing: Whoever was in there with them was on God's side, not Nebuchadnezzar's, and protected them from the fire.

This reminds us of Isaiah 43:2: "When you go through deep waters, I will be with you. When you go through rivers of difficulty, you will not drown. When you walk through the fire of oppression, you will not be burned up; the flames will not consume you."

You might say, "Yes, but Shadrach, Meshach, and Abednego were faithful to the Lord. I haven't been. I've done just about everything wrong a person could do. Why would he care about helping me?"

Remember, God doesn't want anyone to perish, but for all to come to repentance (2 Peter 3:9). He might well let you suffer for your disobedience. That's a big part of how he works (Hebrews 12:5–11). But he's not going to abandon you. If you're a parent, you understand this. You may let your kids learn some lessons the hard way, but you're not going to bail on them. The love that you have for them won't let you.

If you're a pit dweller, there might be several things you need to be concerned about, but God's love for you is not one of them. Nor is his presence in your pit. He's there and he's ready to help.

Stop digging.

There's an old saying we know you've heard: "The definition of insanity is doing the same thing over and over again while expecting a different result." If this is true, then we are sorry to say we have counseled a lot of insane people. (Though in fairness, by this definition we have even been insane ourselves from time to time.) We can't explain it, but there is a tendency in humans to repeat the same mistakes over and over again.

We've all seen the emphysema patient puffing on a cigarette. We know that lots of people who are buried in credit card debt just keep flashing that plastic all over town. Every night, bars are filled with people who are looking to pick up someone, even though picking up people in bars has only brought them misery. Many career-minded people just keep working seventy hours a week, even as they watch their spouses and children grow bitter and distant. Some overweight people with dangerous medical conditions take no thought about what they put into their bodies.

Even animals don't do this. If you have an invisible fence installed in your yard, your dog will get jolted a time or two and figure out that he needs to stay in the yard. But we homo sapiens just keep running out into the proverbial street even when we know we're going to get shocked, or worse, run over.

We'll make this really simple: If you are in a pit you have dug, stop digging!

We've heard people say, "I feel like I'm in a bottomless pit." Well, guess what, until you stop digging, your pit *is* bottomless! It just keeps getting deeper and deeper with every shovelful of dirt you throw out of the hole. Some people say, "I feel like I've hit rock bottom." Our response is, "You may feel like you've hit rock bottom, but if you're still digging, you haven't."

But let's be clear about what it means to stop digging.

It means that you *stop digging!*

So many people we've worked with say they're going to stop digging, but they don't really do it. They just rearrange their digging schedule. Like the man with family problems who says he's not going to stay so late at the office anymore. What does he do? He leaves the office every day at five, but brings his laptop home and works in his home office all evening.

If you want to get out of your pit—especially if it's one you dug yourself—it's critical that you make *real* changes, not cosmetic changes. Cosmetics can make you look better, but they don't cure cancer.

Assess and utilize your climbing tools.

There are no two ways about it. Unless you're Superman, getting out of a pit is always going to involve climbing. And unless you're Spiderman and can shoot sticky webs out of your wrists, you're going to need equipment. We have compiled a list of climbing tools that will get you up that wall and out of your pit.

Climbing Tool #1: Repentance

A lot of people think repentance is being sorry for what you've done, and it does have that element to it. But the word really refers to a change of direction. It's doing an about face when going in the wrong direction and heading back the other way. And its importance cannot be overestimated. Jesus proclaimed that the very reason he came to earth was to call sinners to repentance (Luke 5:32). On the day the Church was born in Acts 2, Peter tied repentance directly to salvation (Acts 2:38). And Paul the apostle wrote again and again that people who failed to address and correct the sin in their lives (repent) would not be saved (Romans 8:13, Galatians 5:19–21, and Ephesians 5:5).

I (Mark) remember a fellow who came forward at the end of a Sunday morning service. He and his wife had been having problems in their marriage and seemed to be at a standoff. Everyone, most of all his wife, was surprised when he stepped out and walked to the front of the auditorium as we sang an invitation song. He stood in front of the entire church and confessed that he had had an affair and wanted to come clean and be a different man going forward. He cried and we prayed and the whole church was wiping their eyes and praising God. It was a beautiful example of repentance.

Except that it turned out not to be repentance at all because, while he did indeed end that illicit relationship, within a couple of months his wife discovered that he was involved with yet another woman. Which means that when he came forward in church and got everybody boo-hooing, he wasn't really repenting. He was just cleaning up a mess he'd made and trying to earn some good will points with his wife and the congregation.

You've heard the old saying that if it looks like a duck and walks like a duck and quacks like a duck, it must be a duck. Well, that may be true of ducks, but we're here to tell you that if it looks like repentance and sounds like repentance and feels like repentance, it isn't necessarily repentance. Repentance is quite possibly the most faked thing in the world. People who are in a tough spot know what to say and how to act to take the heat off of themselves. And they do, quite often. And quite convincingly.

But fake repentance will never get you out of your pit. It might fool people and win back some of the favor you've lost with family and friends. But it won't change much about your life because it doesn't change anything about your heart. That is the key. Repentance is not a performance; it is a fundamental, heart-level change that puts you on a radically different path.

Climbing Tool #2: Truth

Satan is a liar and the father of lies (John 8:44). From the beginning of time, he has employed lies to lead people away from God and into trouble. He started with Eve in the garden of Eden (Genesis 3:1–4) and has been doing it ever since. The interesting thing is his bag of lies isn't very big. It doesn't need to be. Almost anyone's life can be wrecked with one or more of the following six lies:

"You can't trust God." (This is the one that got Eve.)

"No one will ever find out."

"You can handle it."

"Everybody does it."

"It's not a big deal."

"You've gone too far."

We've counseled countless people who seemed genuinely befuddled about their pit experience. They ask, "Why am I in this situation? How did I get here? I never wanted my life to turn into such a mess. What did I do wrong?" Ninety-nine percent of the time, the answer is that they believed one or more of these six lies. Right now, if you're stuck in a pit of your own making, we have no doubt that you can look at those six lies and pick out one or more that you fell for.

Here's the good news: The truth will set you free (John 8:32). Jesus said it and everything we have experienced in all these years of ministry confirms it's true.

When I (Joe) first went into the ministry, I was a little worried about the counseling part of the job. I knew people with all kinds of problems would be coming to me for help. I knew some of those problems would be really weird. And I knew I would be on the hot seat: "Okay, Mr. Preacher. You've heard my story. Now tell me how to fix this mess." I wondered if I would be able to do it.

But here's what I learned: Effective counseling is nothing more than telling people the truth. They may not want to hear it. They may not believe it. They may choose to ignore it. But those responses aren't my problem. My job is to love them and tell them the truth.

My particular style of truth telling is to keep it very bottom line. Or as some who know me would say, to be very blunt:

"If you keep drinking, you're going to lose your family."

"If you keep seeing that woman, your wife is going to leave you."

"If you keep nagging your husband, he's going to learn to hate you."

"If you don't give your wife attention, some other man will be happy to."

"If you keep working sixty hours a week, your wife and kids will resent you."

I don't mean to say that I'm harsh with people. I don't believe I am. But I don't beat around the bush either. If truth is the thing that sets us free, then I believe in getting to it as quickly as possible. We can have a conversation about how that truth might be applied, but tiptoeing around the critical issue is not my style.

And it's not only obvious truths like the ones I just mentioned that are important. It's also biblical truth. I've never found a situation into which the Bible doesn't offer some insight. At times, the Bible's comments can be very direct, such as "You must not commit adultery" (Exodus 20:14). In other places God's word is more nuanced, such as in Jesus's parables. The honest truth is, as a counselor, I don't have to be brilliant. I don't have to have a string of college degrees. I just need to have some common sense and know the Bible. The truth that sets us free is not something that only geniuses can find or comprehend.

Here's the key question: What is the truth that will set you free?

You probably already know. I'm guessing others have told you. Maybe they've been telling you for a long time. Or perhaps plain old common sense has told you. But if for some reason you don't know the truth that will set you free, one of your top priorities right now should be to find out. Ask a friend who loves you enough to be honest with you. Talk to your preacher. I suspect there are several people close to you who have suffered themselves because of *your* pit. I'm sure they would be happy to tell you the truth. And get into your Bible. God's word is nothing *but* truth.

Accept it.

Embrace it.

No matter how painful it is.

Because you're not getting out of your pit without it.

Climbing Tool #3: Inspiration

Have you ever noticed that when a successful individual is asked who inspired them, they always have an answer? Never have we heard someone say, "Nobody inspired me. I thought of this idea all by myself and motivated myself to do it without any inspiration from anybody." That just doesn't happen.

Have you ever listened to kids when they're playing whiffle ball in the backyard? You'll hear things like this: "It's the seventh game of the World Series! The bases are loaded with two outs! And Paul Goldschmidt steps to the plate!" And another kid yells out, "And I'm Clayton Kershaw on the mound!" Those kids have heroes who inspire them, who fill their heads with wonderful dreams. Every person who ever put on a big-league uniform did what we just described.

Inspiration is the fuel that drives you and pushes you. It doesn't make hard things easier, but it makes you want to do hard things. It reminds you that, even though what you want to do is hard, it *is* possible.

But does inspiration really help when you're in a pit? Playing baseball in the backyard is one thing, but what about when you've just lost your marriage or suffered a financial disaster?

Here's what you have to remember: There is no pit that has never been climbed out of. Dream up the worst situation you can think of, and we will guarantee you that someone has been in that hole and climbed out. You can't help but see this if you read the Bible. From Genesis to Revelation, people were in all kinds of dire circumstances and came through them in victory. The prophet Isaiah said, "He has sent me to comfort the brokenhearted and to proclaim that captives will be released" (Isaiah 61:1).

Your challenge is to find your sources of inspiration. Yes, there are plenty in Scripture, but you also need to look around and find living, flesh-and-blood people who have made it through the nightmare you're suffering. I (Joe) have always said it would be nice if people wore signs that indicated the pits they had climbed out of. How that would simplify things!

But here's what we've noticed: People who have similar stories and experiences have a way of finding each other. Maybe it's a God thing. All we know is, we've seen it and experienced it ourselves. When you're going through something hard, it's almost a certainty that you will run into someone who was once in the same pit and made it out. It's very similar to that experience you have when you buy a certain model of car in a certain color. You may never have noticed that car before, but once you own one you will start seeing it everywhere. Once you have a certain problem, you will hear about and even meet people who have been through the same thing. When you find such a person, let them inspire you. And again, read those Bible stories about people and their pits.

Climbing Tool #4: Self-Discipline

Romans 8:12–13 is a powerful passage for people in pits. Paul said:

> Therefore, dear brothers and sisters, you have no obligation to do what your sinful nature urges you to do. For if you live by its dictates, you will die. But if through the power of the Spirit you put to death the deeds of your sinful nature, you will live.

He's saying that we all have a choice. We can live by our sinful impulses or not. And whichever we choose will determine our story. The other not-so-minor detail he throws in is that if we choose to discipline ourselves and "put to death" the deeds of the flesh, the Holy Spirit stands ready to help us. That is some awesome pit theology right there.

If you want to climb out of your self-dug pit, you simply must acknowledge the sins you committed when you were digging it. And you must "put to death" those deeds. We love that terminology. Too many people piddle around with the deeds of the flesh. They're like the drunk who says, "I'm turning over a new leaf. I'm going to limit myself to two beers a day." Or they're like the person whose garage is a disaster, so he rearranges a few things to make some room instead of really getting in there and throwing the junk away. If you're just going to piddle and play around with the deeds of the flesh, you'll never get out of your pit. You might get a leg up, but you'll always slide back in.

Trust the promise of Scripture. Through the power of the Holy Spirit, you can—and you must—discipline yourself and put to death the deeds that put you in your pit in the first place.

If you decide that you've had enough of your pit and are ready to climb out, you need to be prepared for an impulse that will strike you just as surely as little birdies go tweet, tweet, tweet. It will strike you hard because Satan will see to it. A little voice in your head will say,

"Maybe you ought to just stay put. Getting out of this pit is going to be really hard. And what happens once you're out? Will you really be able to live like all those annoying super-righteous people? Do you even want to? At least you're used to this pit, and nobody places any expectations on you. That's not all bad!"

Get ready. That thought is coming.

And when it does, your life and eternal destiny will hang in the balance.

Choose wisely.

2

YES, YOU *CAN* FIND JUSTICE IN AN UNJUST WORLD

> *For I, the* LORD, *love justice.*
> *I hate robbery and wrongdoing.*
> *I will faithfully reward my people*
> *for their suffering.*
> Isaiah 61:8

SAFAA FAHMI IS ONE of the greatest ministers and evangelists alive today that you've never heard of. He has no sprawling church building in the high-rent district of some great American city, no cameras on booms swinging around the stage as he preaches, no highly rated TV show, no TikTok videos piling up millions of views, and no best-selling books stacked up on the front table at your local Barnes & Noble.

All Safaa does is lead people to Christ.

In Egypt, a Muslin stronghold, he was leading a Christian church of over a thousand people. He was running vacation Bible school programs that ministered to ten thousand children across a wide area. (Many of our churches in the United States do well to get thirty or forty kids to VBS. Or they have canceled VBS altogether.) He was also teaching marriage classes, which may not seem like a big deal until you understand that in a Muslim country the treatment of women is very different from what we are accustomed to in the United States.

Safaa Fahmi was so successful that some leaders in his denomination became jealous. So jealous that they began looking for something to criticize. And as you know, when nitpicky people are itching to criticize, they will always find something. In this case, they seized on three main things. One, Safaa was young. In their minds, he was too young to know what he was doing. Two, Safaa was teaching that true, biblical baptism is by immersion. (His denomination practiced sprinkling.) And three, Safaa was encouraging his people to take the Lord's Supper weekly. (His denomination thought it should be less often.) For his age and these two perfectly biblical teachings, Safaa was accused of being a heretic and brought up on charges. If this surprises you, go back and read again the life of Christ. He, too, was branded a heretic by religious leaders who were jealous of him, and even killed for it.

Safaa wasn't killed, but he was convicted of heresy and stripped of his role as the pastor of the church where he served. His treatment was as unjust as anything we have ever witnessed. Many of Safaa's friends and associates found themselves looking heavenward with a raised eyebrow and asking, "Lord, what's up with this? Why couldn't you have stopped it? It isn't right that such a thing should happen to such a faithful servant!"

But then a funny thing happened.

With the denominational shackles removed from Safaa's wrists, he started preaching and ministering again. Now, more than twenty-five years later, his own organization, Christian Arabic Services, has established eleven Bible college campuses and started, or helped to start, 541 churches in Egypt, Northern Sudan, Southern Sudan, Australia, Canada, Syria, England, and Iraq.

And to think the denominational leaders who convicted Safaa of heresy thought they were putting him out of business!

We wanted to share Safaa's story at the beginning of this chapter because it sets the table for what we want to say about injustice, a subject that is on everybody's mind these days because there's so much of it.

A teen girl who is a great athlete and has worked hard for years sees her medal taken by a biological male who says he is a female.

A former marine is arrested and charged with crimes for protecting innocent people on a subway from a deranged maniac making death threats.

A woman who refuses her boss's sexual overtures is threatened and eventually let go for "insubordination."

A scammer defrauds an elderly couple and steals their life savings.

A fifty-year-old person is publicly shamed and "canceled" because of foolish statements he or she made as a teenager.

A charity organization collects huge amounts of money, very little of which ever reaches people in need.

A social media company silences a voice they disagree with, even though that voice is speaking truth.

An older employee is "downsized" out of the company so that younger, cheaper labor can be hired.

We could fill up the rest of this book with examples of injustice. They are so common that many who are victimized by it feel hopeless. How many times have you watched a report on the news and then shaken your head and said, "There's just no justice anymore." Or maybe it wasn't a news report; maybe it was something totally unfair that happened to you. Getting angry at injustice is understandable, but before we embrace the idea that justice can't be found in an unjust world, let's do some thinking.

Yes, we do live in a fallen world where bad things are always going to happen (John 16:33). But as the verse at the top of this chapter makes clear, we serve a God who loves justice, and who has made some very specific promises. As long as Almighty God is on his throne, there will always be justice in the world. The trick is to understand some basic truths.

A Game of Whac-A-Mole

One of the big mistakes we make is looking for justice in human-run systems and institutions. We think, for example, that if an organization has a noble mission, it will naturally produce noble results. The problem is that you always have people executing that mission, and people are not just unreliable but often devious and deceitful.

Take the Black Lives Matter Global Network Foundation, for example. When it was established, most people thought, "Well, black lives *do* matter, and if this organization wants to fight racial injustice, that's great." But now, just a few years later, the organization has lost much of its influence and credibility, not because black lives ceased to matter but because the organization's leaders have become embroiled in all sorts of scandals and lawsuits. Specifically, they have been accused by grassroots BLM members of stealing millions of dollars in donations and using donated money to buy multi-million-dollar mansions.

And Christian organizations are no better.

On the very day that we were writing this paragraph, the Guideposts Solutions Firm released a report about sexual abuse by the ministers of a major Protestant denomination. It was a 205-page list of names, allegations with details, and conviction information regarding fifty ministers in the state of Florida alone.[1]

Many people look at reports like these and say, "How terrible!"

We look at them and say, "How predictable!"

Mark it down: The least surprising thing in the world is human corruption.

---

[1] Ryan Callihan, "More than 50 Florida pastors on Southern Baptist Church's list of alleged sexual abusers," *Bradenton Herald*, May 27, 2022, https://www.bradenton.com/news/local/crime/article261865205.html#.

People clutch their pearls and gasp when they hear about some new scandal involving supposedly righteous people. Why? Hasn't God made it clear that this would be the norm? The prophet Jeremiah said, "The human heart is the most deceitful of all things, and desperately wicked" (Jeremiah 17:9). He wasn't just talking about the people you see on the evening news with their hands cuffed behind their backs. He was talking about what we would call "good, church-goin' Christians." Even preachers! Paul said it as succinctly as anyone ever has: "No one is righteous—not even one" (Romans 3:10). Think of the most righteous person you know, that individual you are convinced has angel wings hidden under his or her clothing. God says that person's righteousness is as filthy rags (Isaiah 64:6).

This is why fighting injustice is like a game of Whac-A-Mole. Injustice pops up in one place and you pound it down. But even before you can draw back your hammer, it pops up somewhere else. Over here, over there, all over the place it pops up faster than you can beat it down. Still, people are shocked when injustice happens to them. We couldn't begin to count the times we have sat and listened to counselees pour out their fury: "I can't believe he did that to me!" We are always sympathetic and let them talk it out, but sooner or later we have to say, "Welcome to life in the real world."

The first step in developing the proper attitude toward injustice is to not be shocked by it. Hate it, yes. Fight it, yes. But never be surprised by it.

God Is Sovereign

The second step is to understand that God is sovereign. As psalm 104 shows us, God is the master of creation, he's in charge. He does whatever he wants at all times. He both causes things to happen and keeps things from happening. He orchestrates circumstances to accomplish his will and keep his promises (Romans 8:28). We might influence him through prayer, but even then, we have no power to control him. He calls the shots, period.

John Piper told a story about how when he was in seminary he was so committed to the idea of man's free will that he had all but completely ruled out God's sovereignty. He said that one day he engaged one of his professors in a lengthy discussion of the subject and concluded with what he thought was the ultimate proof of his own sovereignty. He took an ink pen out of his pocket, held it up in front of the professor's face, and dropped it on the floor. "See there?" he said, *"I dropped the pen!"* (As if the God who hung the stars in the sky couldn't have levitated the ink pen if he'd wanted to.) John Piper was very proud of his cleverness. He walked away with a smug little smile on his face. But by the end of the semester, he had completely reversed his thinking. Why? Because in one of his classes he ran smack into Romans 9,[2] which literally

---

[2] John Piper, "The Absolute Sovereignty of God: What Is Romans Nine About?" *Desiring God*, November 3, 2002, https://www.desiringgod.org/messages/the-absolute-sovereignty-of-god.

pounds God's sovereignty into the reader's head with statements like this: "When a potter makes jars out of clay, doesn't he have a right to use the same lump of clay to make one jar for decoration and another to throw garbage into?" (Romans 9:21).

Ah yes, the potter and clay metaphor. It is unquestionably the greatest picture of God's sovereignty there could ever be. Both Isaiah and Jeremiah wrote about it centuries before Paul did (Isaiah 45:9, Jeremiah 18:1–6). Since then, it has been endlessly taught and preached and sung about by God's people. In particular, the church has loved this song, which we grew up singing:

> Have Thine own way, Lord! Have Thine own way!
> Thou art the potter; I am the clay.
> Mold me and make me after Thy will;
> While I am waiting, yielded and still.[3]

In our experience, most people don't think much about God's sovereignty—much less stew about it—until some sort of grave injustice happens. Then it becomes a front-and-center issue. They want to drag God into a courtroom, plop him down in the witness chair, and start firing questions at him.

"Where were you?"

"Why didn't you stop it from happening?"

---

[3] "Have Thine Own Way," by Adelaide A. Pollard. Music by George C. Stebbins. Published in 1907.

"How could you allow such a good person suffer like this?"

"Were you just kidding when you said you would protect your people?"

In our opinion, getting all huffy at God and demanding answers is a pointless exercise. He doesn't owe us an explanation for anything he does or doesn't do. Rather, what we *should* be doing is thinking through the implications of God's sovereignty as it relates to our suffering. Here's a verse of Scripture that has gigantic implications, but we suspect most people don't even know it's in the Bible. It's from a psalm of Asaph: "It is God alone who judges; he decides who will rise and who will fall" (Psalm 75:7).

That verse has God's sovereignty written all over it. It also screams a reminder to every person who suffers injustice: "No matter what happens to you, good or bad, God is going to decide whether you rise or fall."

Imagine a vertical line.

On the left side of the line are all the people that God decides shall fall. On the right side of the line are all the people that God decides shall rise.

Which side of the line would you like to be on?

The right side, of course! You want to be a riser, not a faller.

And here's why:

When God decides you shall rise, you *shall* rise, and no amount of injustice can stop you. Yes, people will still mess with you. The pain they inflict on you will still hurt. It may disrupt your plans or make life harder for you. But it cannot stop you from rising if God ordains that you shall rise.

Let's see how this worked in a real person's life.

The Testimony of Joseph

In Genesis 37–50 we find the story of a right-side-of-the-line guy. Perhaps he was the most admirable right-side-of-the-line guy in the entire Bible because of the faithfulness he showed during an almost unbelievable string of injustices. Let's review them.

Injustice #1: Sold into Slavery

If you're of our generation, you remember the Smothers Brothers. Tom and Dick Smothers were a comedy team that sang folks songs that usually deteriorated into humorous arguments, such as which one of them was their mother's favorite. Dick always lamented, "Mom always liked you best," which Tom then denied. In Joseph's case, his dad, Jacob, really *did* like him best, a fact that became very obvious to his brothers and left them with a bad case of heartburn.

It didn't help matters that Jacob had a fancy coat of many colors custom made and gave it to Joseph. There the older brothers were, wearing their sale-rack, Walmart tunics, while Joseph was strutting around in his Saks Fifth Avenue robe. He should have been wearing hand-me-downs like they'd all had to. But no, he got preferential treatment from Pops.

And those dreams! The cocky little brat had dreams about himself, dreams in which *he* was *their* superior! How dare he even think such things!

Eventually, their anger boiled over. Their first impulse was to kill him, but that seemed like it might be taking things too far. He was, after all, their brother. So they decided to sell him to some Midianite traders instead. They covered up their crime by staining Joseph's fancy robe with goat's blood and pretending he was killed by a wild animal.

Injustice #2: Sold a Second Time

The only thing worse than being sold once would be to be sold twice, and Joseph was. At this point, he was merely a commodity, an asset that his owners used to get what they wanted. Imagine standing in a slave market while prospective buyers walk around you, inspecting you, sizing you up. We do the same thing today when we go to the car dealership. We have no affection for the molded pieces of metal and plastic the car is made of. We only want to "kick the tires" and see if this product is worth the investment. Joseph was young and fit, so he was desirable property.

Concerning this business of Joseph being sold twice, here's a sidebar from our experience as counselors. We've noticed that most people can handle it when some great injustice is done to them. It might take some time to work through it, but most people will be okay eventually. However, when the same injustice happens a second time, recovery is not as certain. Anger, resentment, and even a feeling of being cursed or abandoned by God can start to take hold. If you've ever known a person you would describe as bitter, this is probably the reason. They didn't suffer just one injustice but multiple injustices. Joseph is now sitting on two, and is just getting started.

Injustice #3: Accused of Rape

Something good finally happened to Joseph. Potiphar quickly realized that he was an exceptional young man with great character, so he put him in charge of his entire household, a household that included Potiphar's oversexed wife.

I (Mark) am a big fan of vintage noir fiction from the 1950s. One of the standard characters in the classic noir novel is the femme fatale. The term actually means "disastrous woman." It's a dangerous, seductive female who uses her charms to lure men into her lair, often leading them to a calamitous end. In Genesis we learn that femme fatales have been around for thousands of years because that's exactly what Potiphar's wife was. She was delighted to have a handsome young man—a new plaything—working around the house. It probably took her five seconds after meeting Joseph to decide to seduce him. The thing about femme fatales is that they don't take kindly to rejection. They expect the men they prey on to give in to their charms, and when they don't, they lash out.

So Potiphar's wife put the moves on Joseph. The Bible says she put "pressure" on him day after day (Genesis 39:10). Trust us when we tell you that the word *pressure* is loaded with meaning. She basically pulled everything but the kitchen sink out of her bag of feminine charms and threw it all at Joseph. But, likely for the first time in her life, she struck out. In a truly epic demonstration of wisdom and self-control, Joseph rejected her advances.

You've heard the saying, "Hell hath no fury like a women scorned." It's actually adapted from a line in William Congreve's play *The Mourning Bride*, written in 1697. Perhaps he was thinking of Potiphar's wife when he wrote the words. She felt scorned, and in her hellish fury decided to frame Joseph for rape.

There are some things you can be accused of and not suffer too terribly, but rape is not one of them. Especially when the person who's accusing you of trying to rape her is your boss's wife. That is pretty much the ultimate career killer. And that's how Joseph, a perfectly innocent man, found himself sitting in a prison cell.

Injustice #4: Forgotten in Prison

During his years—yes, *years*—in prison, God blessed Joseph to the extent that the warden put him in charge of running things. We don't mean he was a hall monitor or head of the cleaning crew. We mean he was running the entire prison. We've heard of no other example in history of a prisoner running the prison where he was locked up, but God is full of surprises.

As he served out his term, Joseph gained a reputation as an interpreter of dreams. In one instance, he accurately interpreted the dream of the royal cupbearer, whom Pharaoh had thrown into prison in a fit of rage. In a culture that placed a lot of emphasis on dreams and their meanings, this should have earned Joseph considerable favor. Once released and reinstated, the cupbearer should have pleaded Joseph's case before Pharaoh: "Hey, this guy Joseph down there in the prison, you wouldn't believe how good he is at interpreting dreams. He could probably be a great help to you."

Instead, the cupbearer walked out the prison door and completely forgot about Joseph.

Ouch.

It's bad enough to do something nice for someone and not hear a "thank you." It's mildly hurtful when you help someone and feel that they don't appreciate what you did. But when you've been unjustly sitting in prison for years, and you know that the testimony of someone you helped might get you released, and then that person completely forgets about you, that is a real gut punch.

So let's review:
Sold into slavery by his own brothers.
Sold again on an auction block.
Unjustly accused of attempted rape.
Thrown into prison.
Forgotten about.

But let us not forget: God decides who will rise and who will fall.

Though one injustice after another was perpetrated against Joseph, God was slowly but surely causing him to rise. God blessed him again and again, causing him to gain favor with key people and to be promoted up through the ranks of authority, far surpassing those who should have been way above him on the company org chart. Eventually—even in spite of all the injustices he suffered—he became the most powerful man in Egypt.

Being a Person Who Rises

Being the kind of person God would choose to be a riser is how we find justice in an unjust world. We don't find it by putting up our dukes and slugging it out with all the corrupt people and systems that make such a mess of things in this world. That is a losing proposition from the get-go. People who do it that way end up bitter and angry and miserable. The only alternative that makes sense is to dedicate oneself to being the kind of person God looks at and says, "Yes, that person shall rise." For as Joseph teaches us, when God tabs you to be a riser, no amount of injustice can hold you back. Yes, you might suffer, but the blessings of God will outweigh the suffering.

What we love about Joseph's story is that it makes very clear why God tabbed him to be a riser. Four qualities stand out that obviously drew God's favor.

Quality #1: Personal Righteousness

David said, "For you bless the godly, O LORD; you surround them with your shield of love" (Psalm 5:12). He might well have added, "And if you want to know what it means to be godly, consider Joseph."

There are many moments of godliness in Joseph's story, but the one most people are drawn to is when he resisted Potiphar's wife's sexual advances. She was almost certainly a knockout, for men of great influence like Potiphar always had their pick of the best-looking women. And she was undoubtedly a skilled seductress. We certainly don't believe she was a paragon of purity until the day Joseph was hired and then suddenly lost her morals. It's more likely that she had perfected her seduction techniques through countless affairs and zeroed in on Joseph as her next conquest. Add to this the fact that Joseph was in his twenties, the age when many men struggle to resist sexual temptation, and you have what amounts to a lit match in a roomful of gunpowder.

But nothing happened because Joseph wouldn't let it.

We believe the real test of godliness for any person is resisting the easy sins. The easy sins are what we might call low-hanging fruit. They're the sins we can commit easily, without a lot of effort, and be almost certain we'll never get caught. An affair with Potiphar's wife would have definitely been low-hanging fruit. She was coming on to him like a locomotive running an hour behind schedule and had obviously mastered the art of deceiving her husband. Almost certainly, they would have had their fun and not gotten caught. But still, Joseph said no.

The Bible says, "The LORD will withhold no good thing from those who do what is right" (Psalm 84:11). As God watched Joseph handle the ultimate femme fatale with flawless virtue, his heart must have swelled with pleasure and the desire to bless him.

Quality #2: Patience

Did you notice that a huge part of Joseph's story involved waiting for something good to happen? Those years in prison must have been especially frustrating as the days slowly passed. We think about how agitated people get today when their flight is delayed, or a traffic jam clogs up the roadways, or a package takes longer to arrive than promised, or a car ahead of them takes more than half a second to pull out when the light turns green. Patience is a rare commodity, but Joseph had it.

That's not to say he never felt frustrated. We suspect there were many days in that prison when he felt like pulling his hair out. You see, patience isn't an absence of frustration, it's the ability to stay calm and not give up when you *are* frustrated. Which reminds us of a psalm King David wrote: "Be still in the presence of the LORD, and wait patiently for him to act. Don't worry about evil people who prosper or fret about their wicked schemes" (Psalm 37:7). If ever a man epitomized those words, Joseph did. And God took notice.

Quality #3: Humility

The Bible says that God gives grace to the humble. In fact, it doesn't just say it once, but three times: once in the Old Testament and twice in the New Testament (Proverbs 3:34, 1 Peter 5:5, James 4:6). Call us crazy, but we get the impression that God doesn't want us to miss this fundamental truth: Our humility opens up the spigot of his grace.

It certainly did for Joseph. As you read his story, you never see him complaining that he deserved better treatment. He could have said, "My wicked brothers are living free while I'm living as a slave. I've always done the right thing. This is unjust. I deserve better." Such a statement would be pretty hard to argue with, wouldn't it? Both of us would have raised our hands and said, "Preach it, brother!" But nowhere do we see that kind of attitude in Joseph.

Contrast Joseph's quiet humility with what we see in people today who feel mistreated. The first thing they do is yell and scream about it. The second thing they do is round up some people to help them yell and scream about it. We're not saying it's wrong to protest, but there are times when the best thing we can do as Christians is humbly endure what's happening to us, so we can show the world our faith. Paul and Silas, who sang hymns in their prison cell, immediately come to mind when we think about the importance of humbly enduring persecution so that God might be glorified (Acts 16:25-34). If they'd been angrily banging on the prison walls and screaming protests, would God have sent the earthquake that opened the doors, and would the jailer and his household have felt compelled to accept Christ? We doubt it.

Quality #4: Trust

In Acts 7, Stephen gave a defense of the Christian faith as he stood before the Sanhedrin. His defense included a history lesson, and that history lesson included this powerful statement about the injustices Joseph endured: "These patriarchs were jealous of their brother Joseph, and they sold him to be a slave in Egypt. But God was with him and rescued him from all his troubles" (Acts 7:9–10).

But God was with him.

Again and again, in both the Old and New Testaments, God promises to go through our struggles with us. The question is, do we believe it? When bad things happen, it's easy to believe we've been abandoned. As counselors, we've heard it over and over again from suffering believers: "Where is God? Why isn't he helping me? I feel so alone."

You want to talk about what it means to have your faith tested? This is it. Do you believe God's promises even when it feels like he's not keeping them? Do you believe he's with you when you're not seeing any evidence of his presence? Do you believe he's working things out for you when it looks like everything is going against you? Do you believe he's keeping your enemies under control when it seems like they're out of control?

Joseph passed this test with flying colors. Even a casual reading of his story reveals a quiet confidence, a sincere belief that if he just stayed the course, God would take care of him. The ultimate proof of this comes at the end of Genesis when Joseph in his supreme position of authority met his hateful, conniving brothers face to face. What an opportunity he had as the most powerful man in Egypt to make them pay dearly for selling him into slavery. Instead, he made one of the greatest statements in all of Scripture, and one that proves beyond any doubt that he believed God was with him and overseeing the many years of his struggles. He said, "You intended to harm me, but God intended it all for good. He brought me to this position so I could save the lives of many people" (Genesis 50:20).

Personal righteousness.
Patience.
Humility.
Trust.

Once again, God decides who rises and who falls. Never in the history of the world has he ever seen these four qualities in one of his children and failed to tab that person as a riser. This doesn't mean that every persecuted believer who lives out these qualities is going to become the ruler of a mighty nation like Joseph did. But it does mean that when the end of that person's story is written, he or she will be able to look back and see the hand of God at work, like Joseph did, and recognize that the reward of faithfulness far outweighs the pain of injustice.

This, then, is the justice we long for.

It doesn't come from people but from God.

It doesn't come in a moment but over time.

It doesn't come easy, but it's worth it.

Paul said it better than we ever could. After speaking of the terrible persecution and injustice he and his fellow apostles suffered, even to the extent of being under the threat of death, he said, "That is why we never give up. Though our bodies are dying, our spirits are being renewed every day. For our present troubles are small and won't last very long. Yet they produce for us a glory that vastly outweighs them and will last forever! So we don't look at the troubles we can see now; rather, we fix our gaze on the things that cannot be seen. For the things we see now will soon be gone, but the things we cannot see will last forever" (2 Corinthians 4:17–18)

3

Yes, You *Can* Feel Good About Your Future in a Deteriorating World

Here on earth you will have many trials and sorrows. But take heart, because I have overcome the world.
John 16:33

WE NEVER THOUGHT WE'D see the day that

> the Grammy Awards show would feature a full-blown Satanic ritual.

> our local Target store would be actively promoting gender dysphoria and Satan worship to anyone, but especially to children.

> public school districts would allow drag shows in elementary schools.

> any sane person would believe there are more than two genders.

biological males would be allowed to compete against women and destroy the integrity of women's sports.

doctors who have taken the Hippocratic Oath would—or would be allowed to—perform gender mutilating surgeries on minors.

criminals would be allowed to run rampant through great American cities, looting stores and businesses with no fear of consequences.

in a post-9/11 world millions of undocumented and potentially dangerous people would be allowed to stream into our country and disappear.

good, productive citizens would be harassed and "canceled" because of foolish statements they made when they were teenagers.

statues of significant historical figures who made great contributions to mankind would be torn down because they lived in a less-enlightened time and fit in with their culture.

In 1956, Soviet premier Nikita Khrushchev pounded his fist on the podium while giving a speech to western ambassadors at the Polish embassy in Moscow and said, "We will bury you!" Some people believe the comment was sloppily translated by the American press and that what he really meant was, "We will be present at your funeral." Either way, he was not making a threat of war, he was suggesting that the West, and in particular America, would destroy itself as a result of cultural decay. If he were alive today, we suspect he would point at the growing decadence of our culture and scream, "See! I told you so!"

We don't know a single person of faith—from ordinary churchgoers to top-level influencers—who isn't sick about what's happening in our country. Depravity that was once unthinkable is now common. Behaviors that were once whispered about in the shadows are now celebrated in the spotlight. And children, who were once considered off limits, are now in the crosshairs as practitioners of the most vulgar sins imaginable see an opportunity to groom and indoctrinate the next generation.

Is it any wonder so many people feel utterly hopeless? We talk to them all the time, people who are genuinely afraid of what's coming, not only for themselves but for their children and grandchildren. We've spoken to young couples who question the wisdom of bringing kids into a world that preys on children like never before. And like you, we hear candidates on both sides of the aisle delivering sound bites and stump speeches that speak of great hope and a bright future, but we don't know a single person who really believes this snowball that is rolling downhill is suddenly going to stop and start rolling uphill, no matter who is elected to public office.

The degree to which people are worried can be seen in the fact that in 2024, "43% of adults say they feel more anxious than they did the previous year, up from 37% in 2023 and 32% in 2022. Adults are particularly anxious about current events (70%) — especially the economy (77%), the 2024 U.S. election (73%), and gun violence (69%)"[4] Yes, anxiety disorders can have many causes, but a common one is worry. And then there's suicide, often attributed to a feeling of hopelessness. In 2022, more than 49,000 Americans killed themselves, but a whopping 13.2 million seriously considered it.[5] No wonder the well-known Baptist pastor Robert Jeffress, when he wrote a book about how Christians should respond to our deteriorating culture, called his chapters "Survival Tips" and titled chapter one, "Don't Panic!"[6]

If you feel panicky when you look around you, and are convinced that you can't feel good about your future in such a rapidly imploding world, this chapter

---

[4] "American Adults Express Increasing Anxiousness in Annual Poll; Stress and Sleep are Key Factors Impacting Mental Health," American Psychiatry Association, May 01, 2024, https://www.psychiatry.org/news-room/news-releases/annual-poll-adults-express-increasing-anxiousness.

[5] CDC National Vital Statistics System (NVSS), July 18, 2024, https://www.cdc.gov/suicide/facts/data.html?CDC_AAref_Val=https://www.cdc.gov/suicide/suicide-data-statistics.html. The number of suicides is undoubtedly higher because many suicides appear to be accidental when they are intentional, such as when a car slams into a tree.

[6] Robert Jeffress, *Courageous* (Grand Rapids: Baker Books, 2020).

is especially for you. We want to share four incredible truths that are guaranteed to put a smile on your face.

Truth #1: God has established pathways to blessing that will never be closed.

No matter what happens around us—no matter how sick and depraved our culture becomes—God has promised to bless his people. And this is no ambiguous promise that has to be interpreted from fuzzy inferences embedded in confusing passages of Scripture. Not at all. God's promises to bless his children are as plain and obvious as the sun in the sky. In particular, he has opened four pathways to his blessings.

Pathway to Blessing #1: Righteousness

David wrote, "For you bless the godly, O LORD; you surround them with your shield of love" (Psalm 5:12). These beautiful words gain much of their power from the fact that David wrote them. If they'd been written by some fat cat who lived in the lap of luxury and never saw hard times, they would be meaningless. David, while he did become a king and was well acquainted with the trappings of royalty, also knew danger and hardship. He was bitterly hated by King Saul, who saw him as a threat to his throne. He lived for some time with a price on his head, hiding out in the surrounding caves and hills. On one occasion, he narrowly escaped assassination when a spear whizzed past his ear and stuck in the wall (1 Samuel 19:10). Even his wife Michal warned him, "If you don't escape tonight, you will be dead by morning" (1 Samuel 19:11).

Some might say, "It sure doesn't sound like God was blessing him."

But wait! Think again!

Yes, David was under duress. But the people who were chasing him never caught him. The hiding places he chose provided security. The plots that were launched against him all failed. The spear that was thrown at him missed. We could go on, but you get the idea. Later in life, when David reflected on these events, he didn't see problems, problems, and more problems. He saw the hand of God blessing and protecting him as he went through those problems.

Note this about all of God's promises to bless the righteous: He never says he will prevent them from having to face problems and difficulties. Not one time. He only says that he'll be there when the fur flies, that his righteous children will be blessed as they go through whatever they go through. Does this mean the heat won't be quite as hot as it otherwise would be? Does it mean the enemy's evil plots will fail? Does it mean the spear thrown in a fit of rage will miss? It can mean these things and so much more. We have no way of knowing how often and in how many ways God protects and blesses us. We think our struggles are so difficult, but we have no idea how much more difficult they would be without God's blessing.

We love what David said late in his life, as he reflected on all that had happened to him: "Once I was young, and now I am old. Yet I have never seen the godly abandoned or their children begging for bread" (Psalm 37:25).

As you live your life in a depraved world, commit yourself to righteousness. Take the Bible seriously. Live a godly life. If you do, you *will* be blessed.

Pathway to Blessing #2: Generosity

For many, many years, the two of us served in different churches in different towns but in the same role (lead minister). The fact that our experiences were often identical is a testament to the fact that people are the same wherever you go. A case in point would be the myriad counseling sessions we had with people who were struggling financially. Overspending, credit card debt, the loss of a job, unexpected repairs, you name it...the stories were pretty much all the same. Including the fact that the counselees, while going under financially and desperately groping for a lifeline, were not tithing. Every time, we would listen to them pour out their anxiety, show some compassion, ask a few questions, and then steer the conversation toward God's promises regarding giving: "Give and it will be given to you" (Luke 6:38 ESV).

"Blessed are those who are generous" (Proverbs 22:9).

"The one who plants generously will get a generous crop" (2 Corinthians 9:6).

"If you help the poor, you are lending to the LORD—and he will repay you!" (Proverbs 19:17).

Then we would say this: "You know, if you want God to bless your finances, you've got to manage them the way he asks you to, and part of that is giving generously." And then, just about every time, the excuses would begin:

"I only make minimum wage. It's hard for me to tithe when I make so little."

"I know I should be tithing, and I'm going to as soon as I get my car paid off."

"I want to tithe, but we promised the kids we'd go on a family vacation this year."

Here's the unvarnished truth: Every time you make a stewardship decision that violates God's word, you are saying to God, "I don't care about your blessings. You can keep them. I'd rather go ahead and do things my way and continue to struggle." Millions of people who think of themselves as good Christians do this every day.

We challenge you to be different. Recognize that God has offered you this pathway to blessing that will never be taken away, no matter how dark and forbidding the world around us becomes. Quit making excuses and tithe! The prophet Malachi said, " 'Bring all the tithes into the storehouse so there will be enough food in my Temple. If you do,' says the LORD of Heavens Armies, 'I will open the windows of heaven for you. I will pour out a blessing so great you won't have enough room to take it in!' " (Malachi 3:10).

Pathway to Blessing #3: Ministry

When you're in ministry for many years like we have been, you eventually deal with every verse in the Bible through your preaching and teaching. In case you're wondering, that would be 31,102 verses. It's interesting how some of them—even some of the most famous verses—float right on by and make little impact, while others, which are more obscure, grab you and won't let go. One fairly obscure verse that really speaks to us (and probably most preachers) is Proverbs 11:25: "Those who refresh others will themselves be refreshed." That verse is God's promise that people who are generous with their time and resources and minister to others will get a blessing in return.

We aren't experts on very many things, but we are experts on the blessings that come from ministering to others. Those blessings are numerous, but two in particular are worth mentioning here.

One is the *relationships* that develop. When you help people, they love you, pure and simple. When they're sick with worry and you take the time to encourage them or pray with them, when you go out of your way to help them out of a jam, when you offer a few bucks when they're a little short, when you sit and listen to them vent when they're having a really bad day, when you have their back as others are attacking them, they will love you. It's not complicated. We can both testify that some of our closest friends today are people we first met when they needed help, and we reached out.

Another blessing that comes from helping people is *inspiration*. We have worked with countless people who were hit by some devastating life circumstance. We show up on the scene thinking that we're bringing a blessing to them, and they end up blessing us way more.

I (Mark) will never forget the day I went to a visit a woman who had just been diagnosed with terminal cancer. She was a great lady and a good friend, but I wondered what kind of emotional state she would be in when I arrived. I needn't have worried. When I walked up to her front door, I saw a big handwritten sign posted on it. It said:

> Thank you for stopping by. Before you knock, know this: I will not allow any sadness in this house. If you came here to cry with me, please be on your way. I am not crying because I am saved and going to heaven. I have nothing to cry about. On the other hand, if you want to come in and laugh and celebrate with me, then please knock.

That is one of the most inspirational things I have ever seen. Many, many years have passed since then, but I still think about the tingle I felt when I walked up and read that sign. It's very common for people who minister to walk away with a bigger blessing than the one they left behind.

Granted, ministry isn't always that easy. You can find yourself in some messy situations with people who are emotional and struggling and sometimes very angry. But neither of us feel that we have given more than we have received. If you want to be blessed in these dark days, reach out and help someone.

Pathway to Blessing #4: Faithfulness

Hebrews 11 is often called the roll call of the faithful.

It could just as accurately be called the roll call of the blessed.

Abel, Enoch, Noah, Abraham, Sarah, Isaac, Jacob, Joseph, Moses, Rahab, Gideon, Barak, Samson, Jepthah, David, and Samuel are mentioned in the chapter. If you placed the blessings they received from God one on top of the other, the stack would reach to the moon. And the reason is because they were faithful. Not perfect, but faithful. They hung in there when things were hard and got up off the deck when they stumbled and fell. They forged ahead in faith, even when they had lots of questions. And they didn't give up when things went sideways. In return, God led them, provided for them, prospered them, gave them children, led them in battle, protected them from their enemies, and answered their prayers.

David, who is one of the faithful and blessed mentioned in Hebrews 11, wrote something interesting in Psalm 103. He said, "Let all that I am praise the LORD; may I never forget the good things he does for me" (Psalm 103:2). David recognized how blessed he was and that those blessings came from God. He wasn't like so many people who take credit for their own good fortunes: "I've worked so hard. I deserve this!" Instead, David said, "He fills my life with good things" (Psalm 103:5). And he was under no illusions as to why God blessed him so. He said, "For his unfailing love toward those who fear him is as great as the height of the heavens above the earth" (Psalm 103:11).

Toward those who fear him.

Toward those who are faithful.

Nothing has changed. God loves to bless people who are faithful.

The bottom line is this: Yes, the world—and our culture—is deteriorating. Some might even say disintegrating before our very eyes. But God's four pathways to blessing are still open. If you are righteous, generous, ministry-minded, and faithful, your life is going to be better than it would otherwise be.

But we're only just getting started.

Truth #2: God walks with us through every circumstance.

The prophet Micah wrote, "The LORD has told you what is good, and this is what he requires of you: to do what is right, to love mercy, and to walk humbly with your God" (Micah 6:8). We think what this verse *doesn't* say is significant. It *doesn't* say: "This is what he requires of you: to do what is right, to love mercy, and to humbly ask God to walk with you."

See the difference?

Whether or not we walk with God doesn't depend on God; it depends on us. We don't put in a request and hope he says yes. We don't sit and wait while he reviews our application and decides if we're worthy. His willingness has already been established. He *wants* to go through every circumstance of life with us and to give us what we need every step of the way. David said, "Even when I walk through the darkest valley, I will not be afraid, for you are close beside me" (Psalm 23:4).

But ultimately, the choice is ours. God does not force his way into our lives. A great example of this is found in Isaiah 30. During the years of wandering in the wilderness, God made it clear to the Israelites that they needed to stick close to him. He said, "Only in returning to me and resting in me will you be saved. In quietness and confidence is your strength" (Isaiah 30:15). But the leaders of the Israelites stepped away from God and tried to negotiate an alliance with Egypt. They saw it as a wise political move, as if just having God with them wasn't enough. They even traveled through a snake-infested wilderness to strike a deal, but later on discovered that the agreement was a sham (Isaiah 30:6-7).

Imagine God sitting back, watching these events unfold. We can see him shaking his head and saying, "What do they think they're doing? *I'm* the one who loves them. *I'm* the one who has promised to take care of them. What do they think they're going to get from the Egyptians that they can't get from me?"

Nothing much has changed. God's offer to walk with us through every circumstance still stands. James said, "Draw near to God, and he will draw near to you" (James 4:8 ESV). Yet countless Christians wander away from God and make alliances with the world. We devour our X or Instagram feed or park ourselves in front of a twenty-four-hour cable news channel while never opening our Bibles. We play games on our phones for hours at a time. We watch mindless (and vulgar) movies and sitcoms but can't find the time to do a daily devotion or prayer time. And we have our favorite politicians that we somehow think are going to save the world. We consume healthy foods and do our daily workouts for our physical hearts but rarely think about our spiritual hearts. We are, in essence, making alliances with Egypt while ignoring our God, who has far, far more to offer.

If you want to feel good about your life and your future, stop making alliances with the very world that is the problem and start walking with God. No, the world won't get any better if you're walking with God, but *your situation* will be much better. Your head will be clearer, and your heart will be lighter. Having his word to be a light to your path and his Holy Spirit to comfort and guide you are not small blessings. We have never seen a Christian who was walking closely with God be panicky and fearful over the state of the world. Concerned, yes. But not panicky and fearful.

Truth #3: God excels at bringing good out of bad.

"We know that God causes everything to work together for the good of those who love God and are called according to his purpose for them" (Romans 8:28). This is one of the most hopeful and beloved verses in the Bible. With the possible exception of John 3:16, it might be the most memorized and quoted verse in the Bible. Who doesn't love it?

But think about this: As beloved as this verse is, it would quickly fall out of favor if we never saw God actually doing what the verse says. The reason this verse is on everyone's lips is because we can look around and see that Paul wasn't pulling our leg when he wrote it.

Allow me (Joe) to tell you about Kathy Davis, a member of Tomoka Christian Church.

Kathy was born visually impaired. When she was just two years old, her parents noticed that when she dropped something she tended to feel around on the floor for it instead of just quickly picking it up. They had her vision checked, and, sure enough, she had scar tissue on both of her retinas. Surgery was not an option, so the family moved from Georgia to Tallahassee, Florida, so Kathy could attend a special K-12 school where she had access to large print materials. She had good peripheral vision but never could read standard print without magnification. Kathy graduated from high school and enrolled at Florida State University where she enjoyed an active college life—leader in her sorority, worshiping in her local church, engaging in lots of fun time, and hours and hours of studying, often with a sighted reader. Kathy was determined to excel, and did. Regretfully, Kathy lost her beloved mother to cancer at the beginning of her senior year. This was devastating since Kathy's mother had been such a powerful source of love and support. Kathy went on to earn her master's degree, got married, and was blessed to have three healthy children.

It was when she was thirty-four that she was dealt a devastating blow.

She started noticing that her already-impaired vision was getting worse. When she visited a specialist, she could tell he was concerned. The conversation went like this:

"You don't think I'm going completely blind, do you?"

"Yes, I do."

"But I can't. I have too much to do. I have a family and children to raise. What am I going to do?"

"I don't know."

Canceling Can't

Kathy says the words "I don't know" were the emptiest, darkest, most hopeless words she had ever heard.

But there was more suffering to come.

It wasn't long before her husband left, making her a blind single mom. Then when she was forty-eight, she was diagnosed with a brain tumor, which required a seven-and-a-half-hour surgery to remove. There was no guarantee that Kathy would survive the surgery, or that she would come out of it with her mind and personality intact. Kathy always knew, though, that God was in control, and her faith was unwavering. It is no exaggeration to say that Kathy Davis was subjected to more suffering in fifty years than most of us would see in three or four lifetimes.

But that's not the whole story. Let me now review what God was doing throughout those years.

Yes, Kathy was visually impaired, but wonderful parents, teachers and pastors made all the difference.

Yes, Kathy's husband left her, but God brought a new man into her life—Tom Davis—who was to become the love of her life, her soulmate. They were so happy on all fronts. Both were employed at Daytona State College, heavily involved in volunteerism, and active in Tomoka Christian Church. Then the worst happened. Tom was diagnosed with ALS, Lou Gehrig's Disease. Another devastating blow for Kathy, who ultimately became Tom's caregiver until his death.

Yes, Kathy went completely blind, but those words from her doctor, that he didn't know what she could do, served as the impetus for Kathy to start the Center for the Visually Impaired (CVI) in 1989 in Daytona, Florida. It was a place where those with vision loss could go to take classes and learn independent living skills.

Yes, CVI was a great service, but God still wasn't done. When the nearby Conklin Center for the Blind and Multi-Handicapped was floundering, God opened a door for CVI to merged with it, and the Conklin-Davis Center for the Visually Impaired was born. Today, there is nothing like it anywhere. It is the premier place for the visually impaired to go for help.

As we interviewed Kathy for this book, she said, "When my doctor told me I was going blind and that he didn't know what I should do, I was inspired to make sure no other person would ever have to hear those same words. I wanted to create a service for the blind that would be the definitive answer for people like me—those who needed to acquire the crucial skills needed to live with blindness. I sometimes tear up when I think of what God was doing all through my life journey. I believe God carved out this particular path for me so I could make a life-changing impact for blind people. As for my own situation, I enjoy being active with my beautiful guide dog by my side. Whether hanging out with family and friends, listening to a good book, worshiping at Tomoka Christian Church, or doing all I can to further the success of CDCVI, I am greatly blessed! I give God all the glory for anything I have accomplished. You don't have to have vision to be a visionary. I'm not blind; I just can't see!"

The promise of Romans 8:28 is not just for Kathy Davis. It's for you, too. If you're a Christian, you may suffer, but God will always be working for your ultimate good. Here are two simple pieces of advice:

First, keep the big picture in view. When you're going through difficulty, God doesn't generally dump mountains of blessings on you all at once. He helps you here and there as needs arise. He gets you through whatever is in front of you. Then, like Kathy Davis, one day you look back at the big picture and see that God's blessings were innumerable.

Second, remember that some blessings come disguised as hardships. Kathy's darkest moment (when the doctor told her he had no idea what she should do) was actually the thing that ignited the great passion of her life. Would she have become what she became, would she have accomplished what she did without hearing those devastating words? No one knows for sure, but it seems doubtful. Don't be surprised if something similar happens to you, that years after what you thought was the worst thing that could happen turns out to be the best.

Truth #4: God is preparing a place for us.

Jesus said, "Don't let your hearts be troubled. Trust in God, and trust also in me. There is more than enough room in my Father's home. If this were not so, would

I have told you that I am going to prepare a place for you? When everything is ready, I will come and get you, so that you will always be with me where I am" (John 14:1–3).

I (Joe) love to explore caves. I don't mean with a tour group. I'm talking about crawling around in places where there's no marked path, no signs pointing the way, no handrails, and no guarantees. Some would say I'm crazy, but spelunking is actually gaining in popularity. We love to think about the wonders of nature on the surface of the earth, but there are breathtaking wonders under the surface too.

There are two things I have learned as a result of my cave explorations. One is that there is no darkness as dark as what you find deep in a cave. And the second is that there is no exhilaration like what you feel when you're crawling around down there in that total darkness and see a small ray of light indicating the way out. You've heard the expression, "My heart leaped." When I have been underground for a while and I see that ray of light, my heart doesn't just leap, it does flips and somersaults and cartwheels.

That's the kind of exhilaration we should feel when we read Jesus's words about heaven. Here we are, stuck in this dark, dark world, but there is a ray of light: the promise that Jesus is right now preparing a place for us, a place where there will be no more death or sorrow or crying or pain (Revelation 21:4).

You might say, "But how does that help me now?"

To answer that question, we'll quote Alexander Chalmers, a Scottish doctor who gave up practicing medicine to become a journalist way back in the 1700s. He is credited with the following quote: "The three grand essentials of happiness are something to do, someone to love, and something to hope for." Interestingly, Christianity offers all three. But right now, our focus is on that last phrase: "something to hope for." For believers, heaven is just that. It wouldn't matter how much we had to do to keep us busy or how many people we had around us to love. If we had no future beyond this dark, rapidly deteriorating world, there would always be a sense of futility hanging over everything.

We have both preached many funerals, and we can tell you there's a vast difference between a funeral for someone who believed death is the end of everything and a funeral for someone who believed there was a heaven to look forward to. I (Mark) once watched as two funeral directors physically pulled a grieving woman off of her husband's embalmed body as it lay in the casket. She was literally trying to get inside the box with his corpse. They were preparing to close the casket for the final time, and, as an unbeliever, she simply could not stand the thought of never seeing him again.

On the other hand, when people believe they will be able to see their loved ones again in heaven, it makes all the difference. You get tears, yes, because of the temporary time of separation and the drastic changes in routine. But you also get smiles and joy and a sense of peace. The apostle Paul said that Christians do not grieve like people who have no hope (1 Thessalonians 4:13). We don't *live* like people who have no hope either.

Again, there are pathways to blessing that are always open to us.

There is the abiding presence of God day by day.

There is God's promise to work for our good in every situation.

And there is heaven to look forward to.

We're not trying to con you into believing the world isn't messed up. It is, and how. But all is not lost. Despair need not be your default outlook on life. There's a lot going on in the spiritual realm to feel good about, even as you read these words. It may look like everything is caving in, but God is working *for* you right this very moment. Never forget what Jesus said to worried people in his generation: "Look at the birds. They don't plant or harvest or store food in barns, for your heavenly Father feeds them. And aren't you far more valuable to him than they are?" (Matthew 6:26).

Yes, you *are* more important to God than the birds that he so faithfully takes care of. And that's why you can always feel good about your future, even in a deteriorating world.

We'll leave you with a beautiful promise of God from Isaiah:

When you go through deep waters, I will be with you. When you go through rivers of difficulty, you will not drown. When you walk through the fire of oppression, you will not be burned up; the flames will not consume you. For I am the LORD, your God.(Isaiah 43:2–3)

4

Yes, You *Can* Live Courageously in a Terrifying World

God has not given us a spirit of fear and timidity.
2 Timothy 1:7

GUAYAQUIL IS THE SECOND largest city in Ecuador. A number of years ago, I (Joe) was there with my friend Mark White to find a site for a new church plant and vet a prospective pastor. We had completed our work and were at the airport preparing to leave the country when one of the scariest situations I've ever been in occurred.

It so happened that every American Airlines plane had been unexpectedly grounded pending inspections. This meant that many hundreds of American Airlines ticket holders were stranded in the terminal with no idea when they might be able to board a flight and be on their way. For a while they remained cool. But as the hours started to pile up, their collective frustration morphed into anger and then into white hot rage. As Mark and I were strolling through the concourse, a full-scale riot broke out. People had had enough.

I hope you've never been in the middle of a riot. If you have, you know how terrifying it is. People tend to lose all judgment as a mob mentality takes over. In this case, they started yelling and screaming and destroying things, even breaking down walls and partitions. If this wasn't scary enough, armed soldiers in riot gear started pouring into the area.

Mark and I had both seen all kinds of riots on television and in the movies. Let me tell you, it's different when you're in one. As we looked for a place to take cover, Mark shouted something we have since laughed about many times. He said, "I don't speak Spanish, but the guns are over there, so let's go *that* way."

I choose only the most brilliant people to be my friends.

All kidding aside, life is full of scary moments. It was true thousands of years ago when our earliest ancestors went out to hunt supper and ran into a hungry T-rex, and it's still true today. In fact, we don't believe the most ill-tempered T-rex could hold a candle to some of the human monsters we have to contend with.

And they're everywhere.

Did you know that one out of every three people you pass on the street has a criminal record?[7] That doesn't mean they're all dangerous, but many are. According to the FBI:

---

[7] Ariana Freeman and Jan Crawford, "Facing a stigma, many ex-convicts in the U.S. struggle to find work, CBS News, January 31, 2023, https://www.cbsnews.com/news/ex-convicts-u-s-struggle-to-find-employment/.

A violent crime is committed every 24.6 seconds.
A murder is committed every 30.5 minutes.
A rape is committed every 3.9 minutes.
A robbery is committed every 1.7 minutes.
An aggravated assault is committed every 39 seconds.
A burglary is committed every 22.6 seconds.
A car is stolen every 40.9 seconds.[8]

To paraphrase author Michael Thompson, dragons and lions are on the loose everywhere.[9] And we do mean *everywhere*. Even in church you will find the wolves in sheep's clothing Jesus talked about, people who are not what they seem (Matthew 7:15). Specifically, he was talking about false prophets, but "prophets" are predators more often than you might think. According to notinourchurch.com, in the average American congregation of four hundred people, there are, on average, seven women who have experienced clergy sexual misconduct.[10]

But as frightening as these stats are, they don't include what might be the scariest moments of all:

When a layoff leaves you with no income and hungry mouths to feed.

When your doctor gives you a life-threatening diagnosis.

---

[8] "2017 Crime in the United States," Department of Justice, https://ucr.fbi.gov/crime-in-the-u.s/2017/crime-in-the-u.s.-2017/topic-pages/crime-clock.
[9] Michael Thompson, *King Me* (Zoweh, 2023), 71.
[10] http://www.notinourchurch.com/statistics.html.

When you are hatefully targeted for your faith.

When your spouse has an affair.

The blunt truth is, we live in a terrifying world. It's no wonder so many people are depressed or suffering from anxiety, and no wonder why so many people believe true courage is out of their reach. They would rather shrink their lives down to practically nothing than get out into the world and live. I (Mark) once knew a lady who was terrified of driving in Orlando traffic. She wasn't old. She had great vision and reflexes. She had driven in small towns for years. But the very idea of venturing out into city traffic like most people do gave her a panic attack. She once told me that if it weren't for her husband (who was able to take her places), she was sure she would be a recluse.

How about you?

Has fear shrunk your life? Are there things—normal things—you don't do, places you don't go, activities you don't participate in simply because of fear?

Does worry have you on edge? Does your mind constantly churn out disaster scenarios? Have there been times when you agreed to do something but then backed out because you started imagining all the things that could go wrong? Are there things you would secretly love to do but don't because you're afraid? And do you pretend that you have no interest in them to hide your fear?

What about trust? Are you so afraid of being disappointed or betrayed that you steer clear of any kind of intimacy? Do you allow bad experiences from your past to keep you from venturing out and trying again? As preachers we've heard this statement countless times: "I don't go to church because I had a really bad experience in church a few years ago." This, too, is fear.

If any of the above describes you, read on.

Peter, a Study in Courage

Of all the Bible characters not named Jesus, we think Peter has as much to teach us about courage as anybody. In particular, there are four key moments in his life—three great and one not so great—when courage, or the lack of it, played a major role.

Key Moment #1: Walking on Water

In Matthew 14, we read about Jesus immediately after the feeding of the five thousand telling his disciples to cross the Sea of Galilee while he goes up into the hills to pray. While the disciples were on the water, a storm rolled in. Not just any storm, but a big ol' hairy storm with claws and fangs. It was so rough that the Bible says the disciples were "in trouble" (Matthew 14:24). This is quite a statement considering that there were professional fishermen in that boat who had survived more than their share of storms.

At three o'clock in the morning Jesus came to them walking on the waves. They thought he was a ghost and cried out in fear. But Jesus calmed them by saying, "Don't be afraid. Take courage. I am here" (Matthew 14:27).

Then Peter makes one of the most astonishing requests, not just in all the Bible but in all of history: "Lord, if it's really you, tell me to come to you, walking on the water" (Matthew 14:28). Jesus does just that, and Peter steps out of the boat onto the waves.

And doesn't sink!

Yes, we know that he eventually *does* start to sink when he takes his eyes off of Jesus, and we will deal with that later. But let's just pause for a moment and give this guy some props. It took some real faith, some real courage to step out onto those waves. We can criticize Peter for taking his eyes off of Jesus, but as I (Mark) once heard an old preacher say, "Peter is still the all-time world champion water walker in the history of mankind."

Key Moment #2: Speaking Truth to the Jews

Both of us have been preachers for a long, long time. We've preached thousands of sermons, and we can tell you that while all good sermons have hard truths in them, some truths are harder than others. Sometimes you just know that what you have to say isn't going to sit well with some people. We've both had people get up and walk out in the middle of our sermons because they didn't like what they were hearing. And when they walk out, you know that's just the beginning. They're then going to broadcast their displeasure far and wide, telling whoever will listen about that awful, hurtful, judgmental preacher who is offensive and doesn't have the love of Jesus in his heart. This is why there's so much milquetoast, namby-pamby preaching in our world. It takes courage to tell people the truth.

On the day of Pentecost—the day the church was born—Peter stood up to preach and took the "hard truth" reality to the next level. We could analyze his sermon for pages, but we'll just cut to the chase. He told his listeners, the Jews, that they were murderers: "So let everyone in Israel know for certain that God has made this Jesus, whom you crucified, to be both Lord and Messiah!" (Acts 2:36). In other words, God sent the Messiah we've been waiting for, and you murdered him.

Key Moment #3: Defying the Sanhedrin

If some people's feathers were ruffled by Peter's bold sermon, that was not the primary response. The primary response was that people started accepting Jesus right and left. Thousands were baptized, and the infant church was off and running, a fact that gave the Jewish leaders a bad case of heartburn. They promptly arrested Peter and John and threw them in the clink overnight (Acts 4:3). The next day they brought the two rabble rousers before their assembly and demanded an explanation, and boy did they get one. In fact, Peter repeated his assertion that the very men who were questioning them had murdered Jesus, but that God had raised him from the dead (Acts 4:10).

This left the Jewish leaders in a quandary. They needed to shut Peter and John up to try and squelch this new Jesus movement, but they knew they couldn't get rough with them because the people might riot. So they shook a finger in their faces and warned them to be quiet, prompting Peter (and John) to make one of the most courageous, faith-filled statements in history: "Do you think God wants us to obey you rather than him? We cannot stop telling about everything we have seen in heard" (Acts 4:19).

Preachers today who have bold things to say can console themselves with the knowledge that the worst that will probably happen to them is to be fired. For Peter and John, the potential consequences were much greater. They knew their audience had killed Jesus, so there was no question about the extremes to which they might be willing to go to shut Peter and John up. Even so, they said what needed to be said.

Key Moment #4: Denying Jesus

During the last supper Jesus shared with his disciples, Peter was feeling pretty cocky about his loyalty to Jesus. He boldly proclaimed that even if everyone else deserted Jesus, *he* never would. Jesus predicted that Peter would indeed betray him that very night, not once but three times. The Bible says that Peter insisted he would never betray Jesus, even if he had to die (Matthew 26:35).

We have some sympathy for Peter here. He wasn't lying. He loved Jesus and was saying what he truly believed. His big mistake was not overestimating his devotion to Jesus, it was underestimating his human weakness. Talking around a dinner table is very different from facing a life-threatening situation.

When Jesus was arrested and taken away, Peter followed at a distance, which absolutely took some courage. Give Peter some points for that! What he didn't anticipate was that he would be recognized as a follower of Jesus. A servant girl said, "You were one of those with Jesus the Galilean" (Matthew 26:69). So often it's the unexpected development—the thing we don't anticipate—that does us in. Peter panicked, and in a matter of moments had denied Jesus three times, even cursing in an effort to lend authenticity to his denials (Matthew 26:72). As the dust clears, we see him weeping bitterly, recalling Jesus's prediction.

Peter Preaches About Courage

As far as we know, Peter never stood before an audience and preached a sermon on courage. But his actions in these four situations speak volumes. What follows are seven great truths about courage that Peter teaches us.

Courage Truth #1: Boasting doesn't make you brave.

If you've seen the movie, *Top Gun*, you may remember Tom Cruise's commanding officer lecturing him about his reckless actions in the air. He says, "Son, your ego is writing checks your body can't cash." Jesus could have said those very words to Peter at the last supper. His ego was producing epic boasts. It's as if he believed courage and boasting go together.

On the contrary, boasting is overconfidence, and overconfidence has brought down more favorites and elevated more underdogs than any other factor.

Pat Summitt was arguably the greatest college basketball coach of all time. On one occasion, her team got blown out by a far inferior opponent. She felt the loss happened because her team was too cocky and didn't take the opponent seriously. Coach Summitt didn't just call it "one of those nights" and tell her players to forget it and move on. Instead, she had the score painted in big orange letters on the training room wall. She also had T-shirts made with the score printed on the front and required her players to wear them during practice. She was determined that her team would remember that awful night and learn that overconfidence is just as much their opponent as the other team.

Paul the apostle warned us to be careful when we think we stand, lest we fall (1 Corinthians 10:12). James said that God opposes the proud but gives grace to the humble (James 4:6). Courage begins with a clear understanding of your own weaknesses and vulnerabilities.

And you have them.

We have them.

Everyone has them.

The moment we get cocky, we endanger ourselves.

Courage Truth #2: Heeding a warning doesn't make you a coward.

Jesus's warning that Peter would betray him should have caused Peter to take a step back and do some serious thinking. Instead, Peter puffed up his chest and made the ultimate boast: Even if they kill me, I won't betray you. We've seen this kind of thing happen many times in counseling sessions. Both of us have warned people that their attitudes or actions were going to bring them serious trouble if they didn't make a major course correction:

> "If you don't start spending more time with your family…"

> "If you don't get some help for your drinking problem…"

> "If you don't end that toxic relationship…"

But often, the people we're warning do what Peter did. They scoff and explain why there's really nothing to worry about: "I appreciate your concern, preacher, but don't worry. I have everything under control." In almost every such case, we end up meeting with the person again at some point to help them pick up the pieces of the very disaster they said wouldn't happen.

There are two reasons why we might balk when we hear a warning.

The first is that we see a warning as an attempt to limit or confine us. Teenagers in particular are geared to explore and experience new things, so when their parents caution them and set up boundaries, they feel they're being held back, even deprived. Many teenagers try alcohol and drugs, not because they want to drink and get stoned, but because they want to break down barriers.

A second reason why we might balk at a warning is pride. We want to prove that we *can* handle what someone thinks we can't. We *can* succeed where someone thinks we'll fail. We *can* find happiness where someone thinks we'll find only trouble. We often wonder how many couples get married simply because somebody somewhere told them they weren't right for each other. The wedding was their way of saying, "Oh yeah? We'll show you!"

In epic adventure movies, the hero is often seen defying the warnings of others: "Don't do it! It's too dangerous!" pleads the princess to the handsome knight. He hears the warnings but cannot shrink from the task. With his armor-clad chest out and his Fabian-like locks blowing in the wind, he sets his face toward the likelihood of certain death and charges forward.

Life is not a movie.

Courage does not demand that we ignore warnings.

You can be brave without being stupid.

Yes, there will always be times when it's important to press on in the face of danger, but anytime a person who is wiser, more experienced, or more spiritually mature warns you that you might be headed for trouble, pay attention.

Courage Truth #3: Thoughtful planning breeds courage.

Peter's decision to follow at a distance when Jesus was arrested was clearly made with little or no thought. If he'd taken a moment to think it through, he would have realized there was nothing he could do for Jesus at that point. The best he could hope for was to see where they took him or perhaps discover what they planned to do with him, which he would have found out eventually anyway. We believe the reason he failed so miserably when he was recognized and accused of being a follower of Jesus is because he hadn't thought through what he might do if that happened.

The problem with impulsive actions is that they produce impulsive *reactions* when things go sideways. And impulsive reactions—as in the case of Peter's denials of Jesus—usually make bad matters worse. Consider these statements, which we've all likely made:

"I wish I had that to do over again."

"I don't know what I was thinking."

"I sure learned my lesson."

"I'll never do *that* again!"

We would guess that at least ninety percent of the time when one of these statements is made, it's made in reference to an impulsive action that didn't work out well. An impulsive action that probably wouldn't have been attempted if some serious thought had been given to the situation.

Understand that careful thought and planning breeds courage. When you're heading into a difficult situation knowing that you have carefully considered your options and settled on the one that makes the most sense, you can move ahead with much greater confidence than if you're just flying by the seat of your pants.

In Shakespeare's *Henry IV, Part 1*, the cowardly Falstaff pretends to be dead on the battlefield in order to save himself. He later says, "The better part of valor is discretion." We don't think discretion is the *better* part of valor, but we do think discretion is a plus in most situations, especially those that are dangerous.

About thirty years after his betrayals of Jesus, Peter himself wrote, "prepare your minds for action and exercise self-control" (1 Peter 1:13). Perhaps, as he wrote those words, he was thinking back to the terrible night of his betrayals and how he foolishly and unnecessarily got himself into a hot spot.

Courage Truth #4: Courage comes easier when you're in a group.

You've seen the press conferences that are held anytime there's a great tragedy, such as a mass shooting or a devastating storm. You get the primary official—usually the police chief or the mayor—standing at the microphone, laying out the details of the situation, while in the background, standing shoulder to shoulder behind the spokesman, are the various dignitaries lending support (or maybe just wanting to be on camera).

Something like this happened in Acts 2 on the Day of Pentecost when Peter preached the sermon that launched the Church. We doubt that the phrase "fire and brimstone" had been coined to describe sermons at that point, but it surely made the listeners uncomfortable the way a fire-and-brimstone sermon would because, as we've already pointed out, Peter called the whole lot of them murderers.

I (Mark) was nineteen the first time I preached a sermon in a church other than the one I grew up in. In that sermon, I made some comments about secular education. I had attended a secular college for a year and saw firsthand the difference between it and the Bible college I was currently attending. Right in the middle of my comments a man in the congregation stood up and interrupted me. I would learn later that he was the superintendent of schools for that county. He said, "I know it's popular to trash secular education, but I feel it's my job to defend it." He then went on to sing its praises for two or three minutes while I stood there in shock. I had been to church just about every Sunday of my life but had never seen someone stand up and interrupt a preacher's sermon. Naturally, the people and the host preacher were aghast. They knew it was my first attempt at preaching and felt sorry for me. After the service, practically everybody in the building (except the superintendent) came up to me and apologized for the man's rudeness and begged me not to let his thoughtlessness discourage me.

Talk about getting off to a rocky start!

But here's what I learned: If you say something people don't like in the pulpit, they will not hesitate to let you know. Over the years I've received angry phone calls, nasty letters (some signed and some not), and had people stomp out in the middle of my sermon and badmouth me all over town. Every preacher has these experiences. But I was interrupted right out of the gate.

So back to Peter.

He knew when he stood up to preach that his comments were not going to be easy for the people to swallow. It probably was easier for him to be courageous in that moment because the other apostles were standing with him, backing him up both literally and figuratively. Were they standing shoulder to shoulder behind him like at a press conference today? Probably. But we know they were there, and that's what mattered.

In your quest to live courageously in a terrifying world, realize the importance of community. Sometimes circumstances will demand that you stand alone, but most of the time you will have an opportunity to align yourself with like-minded people who will stand with you and have your back. This will make a tremendous difference.

Courage Truth #5: You're more courageous when you know what God can do.

Peter's water-walking experience is a favorite of pulpiteers everywhere because it offers a double whammy. The preacher can hammer his two favorite themes: faith (stepping out of the boat) and faithfulness (keeping your eyes on Jesus). If you ask any pastor to pick two qualities he'd love to have characterize his people, there's a ninety-nine percent chance he would pick faith and faithfulness.

Let's think about the faith part. Stepping over the side of that boat is one of the most incredible moments in the Bible. We talk about the great firsts in history: first person to climb Mt. Everest, first man to walk on the moon, first man to fly around the world, etc. In our humble opinion, none of those firsts come close to Peter stepping out of that boat expecting to walk on the water. The wow factor is off the charts! But it illustrates an important point: We're always more courageous when we have seen what God can do.

If anyone else in the world had encouraged Peter to step out of the boat, he wouldn't have done it. But because it was Jesus, his mindset was entirely different. No doubt he was saying to himself, "I've seen this guy work miracles. I've seen him heal blindness and leprosy. I've even seen him raise the dead." Knowing for a fact that someone can raise the dead does wonders for your confidence in that person.

So here's an important question: Are you convinced of what God can do? You've probably heard the Bible stories about his miracles, but do you truly believe them? It's one thing to nod your head while the preacher is talking about them; it's another thing to be convinced that such power is real and available to you. The blunt truth is that your level of courage is going to be tied to your level of faith in the power of God.

Here are two quick suggestions on how you can increase your faith.

One, put yourself in the right environment. If you want to grow a rose, you don't put it in the freezer. You put it in the sunlight. If you want to grow faith, put yourself in a place where faith flourishes. Go to church, hang out with people of faith—people who have great testimonies. Join a Bible study or small group. This doesn't guarantee your faith will grow.

But at least you'll be in an environment where your faith *can* grow.

Two, start claiming God's promises. The Bible tells us to "taste and see that the LORD is good" (Psalm 34:8). In other words, don't just smell what's cooking on the stove; get yourself a bowl and scoop some of it up. Don't just take someone's word that God can do great things; let him show you. Remember when Peter had fished all night and caught nothing, but Jesus told him to go back out and let down his nets? Peter didn't want to do it. Who would've wanted to try again after an entire night of futility? But he did, probably with some really bad body language. Soon he was hauling in so many fish his nets were tearing, and his boat was ready to sink (Luke 5:1-11). That's what you call tasting and seeing that the Lord is good. You can do it too. Take God's commands and promises seriously and let him impress you. Then, when you need courage, those memories will give you the boost you need.

Courage Truth #6: You're more courageous when you keep your eyes on Jesus.

We've dealt with the importance of faith, now let's think about faithfulness.

Everything was fine for Peter on those waves. We believe he not only could have walked on them, but he also could have done a little dance or maybe some handsprings. If he had, the other disciples probably would have been piling out of the boat right behind him to share in the experience. Maybe they all would have had a party on those waves. But it didn't happen because Peter let his eyes stray from Jesus and started to sink.

You'll not find us hammering Peter for this. As previously mentioned, he still holds the all-time record for water walking in all of human history. And there have been times when both of us have let our eyes drift away from Jesus in far less frightening circumstances. However, we must point out the truth: The sinking started when Jesus was no longer Peter's focus. His eyes drifted to the waves, and that was all she wrote.

As preachers, we have seen this over and over again. People—sometimes a couple or an entire family—are active in church. They're worshiping and serving and into the word and really growing spiritually. They're walking on the waves, so to speak. Then, for whatever reason (we've heard a million of them!), they drop out of church. And what happens? The sink begins.

It never fails.

We've both seen the deterioration that happens. Cracks start to appear in the marriage. Tension develops. Conversations become clipped and sarcastic. Finances get tight because giving has stopped, and priorities have changed. Kids are more easily influenced by their unbelieving peers. Sometimes the dropouts come crawling back to church, confessing what a tough time they've been through and wanting to get back on track. Sometimes they never come back.

Either way, the truth stands: No one in the history of mankind has ever grown stronger in his or her faith after dropping out of church and getting lazy with the spiritual disciplines. To keep growing, to have courage when you need it, to stay on top of the waves, you *must* stay focused on Jesus, period.

Courage Truth #7: You're more courageous when you keep heaven in mind.

Paul the apostle told us to think about the things of heaven, not the things of earth (Colossians 3:2). We don't believe he means that we should disconnect from life in the real world and live with a kind of distracted, I-can't-be-bothered attitude toward what's going on around us. There are some Christians that do this. There are some *churches* that do this. But Jesus said to go *into* all the world with the Gospel (Mark 16:15). We're not suggesting friendship with the world, which makes you an "enemy of God" (James 4:4), but it's hard to imagine how isolation would ever help us win the world for Christ.

We believe Paul was talking about something else. Call it a mindset.

We live *in* the world. We wear the armor of God. We contend for the faith. We preach the Gospel. We take on the enemy. But we never forget that this world is not our home, that we're only here for a little while. We have heaven on our minds wherever we are and whatever we're doing—especially when life gets hard.

When I (Mark) was in high school, I talked to my dad whenever I was struggling with a momentous decision (like whether I should ask a certain girl out). He always had a stock answer. He didn't try to tell me what to do; he simply said, "So if you do it, what's the worst that can happen? And can you accept that?" I didn't realize at the time what good advice that was. To this day, I find myself reflecting on those two questions when I have a tough decision to make.

In the world's eyes, the worst that can happen is death. As Christians, we can accept that if it happens to be where the road of faithfulness leads us because it means we get to go to heaven. This is not a gimmick or mind game we play with ourselves. It's not some kind of mental backflip that enables us to survive hard times. It is the core of our faith, the reason for our joy. It's what Paul was getting at when he asked, "O death, where is your victory? O death, where is your sting?" (1 Corinthians 15:55). It's a million times easier to be courageous when you know that the worst thing that can happen to you is actually the best thing that can happen to you.

When we met to lay out the content of this chapter, Joe mentioned Peter's death. Tradition says that the Roman Emperor Nero ordered that he be crucified. However, Peter felt he was not worthy to be crucified like Jesus, so he requested to be crucified upside down. If true, in addition to showing his respect for Jesus, he was surely also demonstrating a complete lack of fear of death, as if to say, "Do your worst. I'm going to be just fine."

If you buy in to these seven truths, courage is not going to be your problem. You'll have plenty of it. However, we do want to close this chapter with a word of caution. Always remember that there is, at times, a fine line between courage and foolishness. Sometimes things that look like courage are just dumb, emotional reactions that accomplish nothing and make matters worse.

Remember when Jesus was being arrested and Peter drew his sword and lopped off Malchus's ear? (John 18:10). At first blush, one might say, "Wow! He was so brave!" Actually, he was out of control. His head was in the wrong place, which Jesus pointed out in his response: "Put your sword back into its sheath. Shall I not drink from the cup of suffering the Father has given me?" (John 18:11). Impulsive, thoughtless actions stand a good chance of being foolish and counterproductive. If Jesus hadn't healed Malchus's ear, who knows what might have happened? Being courageous doesn't mean being reckless. Courage that is thoughtfully applied is the best kind of courage there is.

5

Yes, You *Can* Conquer Your Besetting Sin

Resist the devil, and he will flee from you.
James 4:7

IN THE EARLY DAYS of my (Mark's) ministry, long before there were cellphones, I needed to ask the chairman of my elder team a question. Since I was driving past his house, and since his car was in his driveway, I decided to drop in and see if he had a moment to chat. His wife answered my knock and told me to walk around the house, that he was in the backyard working in the garden. Little did I know that something was about to happen that would rock both of our worlds.

When I stepped around the back corner of the house, I saw him with a hoe in his hands, stabbing at the dirt and soaking with sweat. I also saw that he had a cigarette dangling from his lips. When he saw me, he jerked the cigarette out of his mouth and threw it down quickly.

We talked for about five minutes. I asked my question, and he gave me an answer. I thanked him for his time and walked back around the house to my car. I was not thinking about my question or his answer. I was thinking about the cigarette. I'd had no idea he smoked.

I spent the rest of the afternoon and evening trying to process this new information. I'd actually heard this man speak against smoking in casual conversations, saying what a nasty habit it was. Yet there he'd stood, with a cigarette in his mouth. I wondered if he was at his house at that moment, feeling as unnerved as I was. I got my answer bright and early the next morning.

When I arrived at the church office, he was waiting on me. He plopped down in the chair in front of my desk, leaned forward, placed his face in his hands, and wept. In a torrent of words, he told me that he had been fighting his smoking habit his entire life. He said that he'd quit many times, sometimes for more than a year, but always found himself starting back up again. He said he was embarrassed and ashamed of himself. He confessed that he had failed so many times that he had all but given up hope of ever being able to quit. He said, "I've come to the place where I feel like the only thing I can do is try to hide it. But even at that I failed."

We talked for a long time, read some Scripture, and prayed. I moved on from that church shortly after this happened, so I don't know if he ever conquered his habit. But I have never forgotten that incident. It impressed a cold reality on the mind of a young preacher: not all temptations are created equal. Some have the strength of a kitten, while others possess the power and viciousness of a full-grown tiger. In this chapter, we're going to tackle this problem head-on because we know millions of Christians are fighting a private battle against a besetting sin and feeling more hopeless by the day.

Before we proceed, I (Mark) must tell you what Joe said when I told him the story above. He nodded as I talked. When I finished, he quipped, "Oh, that a church's biggest problem nowadays would be a smoking elder." He wasn't trivializing smoking or elders, but he said it because in this generation, Christians commonly struggle with besetting sins that, back in the day, were rarely thought about, let alone talked about. In recent years, we've both had church members who confessed struggles with same-sex attraction, pornography, child pornography, adultery, masturbation, stealing, lying, and gambling, among other things. Not that these sins didn't exist thirty or forty years ago, but the deterioration of our culture has changed things. Talk to anyone who's been counseling people for a few decades as we have, and they will tell you it's a different world out there. A darker world. A scarier world. So many people are in bondage to sin. You'd have to be living on a deserted island not to see it. We have no doubt that some of the people who pick up this book will be at the end of their proverbial rope, clinging by a fingernail to their last thread of hope, a heartbeat away from giving up and letting go.

For that reason, we want to begin with some encouragement.

If your besetting sin has been beating you like a Buddy Rich drum solo, take comfort in the fact that you're not alone. Paul the apostle wrote of his own struggle with sin: "I want to do what is right, but I can't. I want to do what is good, but I don't. I don't want to do what is wrong, but I do it anyway" (Romans 7:18–19). There's also David, the man after God's own heart. He rolled over like a trained seal when he spotted Bathsheba bathing on the roof of the house next door. Many have even called David a womanizer because he acquired wives (eight we know of) and concubines like the two of us used to collect baseball cards (2 Samuel 5:13). Some scholars suggest that David's marriages were mostly political, as if that somehow mitigates his sin. Our view is that both sexual lust and the lust for political power can easily qualify as besetting sins, and one is no better than the other.

The point is, if guys like Paul and David struggled with sin, we shouldn't beat ourselves up if we do. In fact, there is one positive result of struggling with sin. J. C. Ryle said it 150 years ago in his book *Holiness*: "A deep sense of struggle, and a vast amount of mental discomfort from it . . . are healthy symptoms for our condition, and prove that we are not dead, but alive."[11] You may feel defeated, perhaps even dead because of your repeated moral failures. We agree with Mr. Ryle that as long as your failures bother you, you're still kickin'.

For further encouragement, remember that our salvation does not depend on our ability to blow every temptation to smithereens like some video game

---

[11] J.C. Ryle, *Holiness* (Charles Nolan Publishers, 2001), 24–25.

superhero. In fact, even if you *could* become an expert law-follower, vanquishing every temptation that comes down the pike, it wouldn't get you into heaven. Paul said that no one can be made right with God by strictly following the commands of Scripture (Romans 3:20). You have to depend on something else, and that something else is God's grace.

We'll say it again because it's critically important: The reason to conquer your besetting sin is *not* because doing so guarantees your admittance to heaven. It's because a besetting sin stunts your spiritual growth, damages your witness, and steals your joy. The one thing all people who struggle with a besetting sin have in common is misery.

And one more thing about God's grace:

Don't worry about it being insufficient to cover your Godzilla-sized sin. Paul said, "God's law was given so that all people could see how sinful they were. But as people sinned more and more, God's wonderful grace became more abundant" (Romans 5:20). This abundance of grace is not a license to sin (Romans 6:1–2), but it *is* a source of hope and encouragement on those bad days when we are particularly pathetic and weak.

Feeling better?

We hope so. And we hope you're ready now to think seriously about what it's going to take to conquer your besetting sin, whatever it is. Actually, it doesn't much matter what it is because the steps to overcoming all troublesome sins are the same. Let's dig in.

Step One: Prioritize

The definition of the word *beset* is "to trouble persistently," and in that definition we find our first step to success. If a temptation defeats you by persistence, it stands to reason that equal, if not greater, persistence is going to be required to stave it off. Fight fire with fire.

Unfortunately, we've discovered that the degree to which a person wants to overcome a besetting sin can fluctuate from one day, or sometimes from one hour, to the next, greatly affecting his or her level of persistence. For example, in the immediate aftermath of a moral failure when the feeling of guilt is crushing, or when an embarrassing moment has been suffered as a result of our behavior, the desire to defeat the sin is usually off the charts. "I've *had* it with this! I'm going to beat this habit if it's the last thing I do!"

But as time passes and the guilt subsides, and especially if we suffer no harsh consequences, the sense of urgency lessens. We may still wish we could overcome it, but it no longer feels like a desperate need. Hence, our level of determination (which undergirds persistence) wanes. Is this your common experience? If so, you'll probably not be successful until something changes. You simply must prioritize victory every minute of every day.

What does this mean?

It means something has to happen in your heart.

Plenty happens in our heads when we are struggling with sin. After every failure, bitter, angry, agonizing thoughts rush through our minds like water from a broken dam. And those thoughts certainly motivate us in the moment. We tell ourselves this is it; things are going to be different from now on. The problem is thoughts come and go like headlines in a newspaper. No matter how big today's headline is, starting tomorrow it will begin working its way toward the back of the paper until it's gone entirely. So just thinking about what we need to do isn't enough; our heart has to be in it.

The word *heart* appears in the Bible a whopping 826 times, according to *Strong's Exhaustive Concordance*. The reason is because it's in the heart that our true will is found.

Think about that old saying, "Actions speak louder than words." Why do we believe this is true? Because we know our words reveal our thoughts, but our actions reveal what's in our hearts. A man can tell his wife he loves her, but if he then routinely mistreats her, his words mean nothing. Likewise, we can say we want to defeat a besetting sin, but if our sense of urgency cools when the crisis passes, then our words are empty. It's the heart that tells the truth about us, not the tongue. This is why Proverbs says, "People may be right in their own eyes, but the Lord examines their heart" (Proverbs 21:2).

David showed a profound understanding of this in Psalm 51. He was pouring his heart out to God in the aftermath of his disastrous sin with Bathsheba. His thoughts as he prayed were definitely in the right place, but he knew that repairing the damage he had done would take more than just proper thoughts. That's why he prayed, "Create in me a clean heart, O God. Renew a loyal spirit within me" (Psalm 51:10).

So it's time for you to ask yourself where your heart is in this matter of your besetting sin. Sure, it bothers you, but how much? The answer to that question will be seen in what you're willing to do to achieve success.

Step Two: Pray

So much prayer in our world is uttered casually or out of habit with minimal umph behind it. Sometimes we pray like we grab lunch on the run: we make it quick so we can be on our way. We'll be honest. That's not going to cut it here. The Bible says, "The earnest prayer of a righteous person has great power and produces wonderful results" (James 5:16).

The *earnest* prayer, not the casual prayer.

When we think about earnest prayer, we think about Hannah's prayer for a son. The Bible says she prayed so fervently that the High Priest thought she was drunk. Can you imagine? He actually reprimanded her for being tipsy and told her to get off the sauce. She responded, "I haven't been drinking wine or anything stronger. But I am very discouraged, and I was pouring my heart out to the LORD. Don't think I am a wicked woman! For I have been praying out of great anguish and sorrow" (1 Samuel 1:15–16). It's worth noting that God answered her prayer.

But it's not just earnestness God is looking for, it's also righteousness. Notice, James said that the earnest prayer of a *righteous* man has great power. Both of us have sat in counseling sessions and listened to people with obvious, egregious sin in their lives pour out their irritation toward God for not answering their prayers. People cohabitating outside of marriage. People ignoring their families while they become slaves to their work. People spending money on luxuries while not giving a dime to the Lord's work. We'll just be blunt: Don't get your hopes up for a flurry of answered prayers if your lifestyle shows no respect for God and his word. We don't presume to know what God will do in every situation, but we can't think of a time in the entire Bible when his people's blatant disobedience motivated him to bless them.

Beyond earnestness and righteousness, there are two other issues regarding prayer that need to be addressed.

The first is a feeling of unworthiness. When you struggle with a besetting sin—and especially when it's just clobbered you for the umpteenth time—you might have an impulse to pray, but Satan will suppress it by planting all kinds of negative thoughts in your head: "You, pray? What are you doing, trying to become the biggest hypocrite in history? Like God's going to pay any attention to the likes of you, you sinner!" And that will be just for starters.

Don't pay any attention to those thoughts.

Understand that prayer isn't—and never has been—about worthiness. Think about it. Who is really worthy to approach God with a request? The Bible says that our righteousness, even the righteousness of the best among us, is filthy rags (Isaiah 64:6). It also says the heart of man is deceitful and exceedingly corrupt (Jeremiah 17:9). Trust us: nobody is worthy to step before God and start laying out requests. The reason we do it is because he invites us to in his word. Paul said, "Don't worry about anything; instead, pray about everything" (Philippians 4:6). "Everything" just about covers it, right? The good and the bad. Your successes and failures. Your shining moments and embarrassing moments.

You might wonder why God would want you to pray if he already knows everything that's in your heart. It's because, as hard as it may be to believe, he wants to have a relationship with you, and without words there can be no meaningful relationship. Imagine seeing an attractive person on the bus every day as you go to work. You stand at the same bus stop, board at the same time, ride the same route, and even get off at the same corner. But until you have a conversation, it would be dishonest to say you have any kind of meaningful relationship. You could say you spend a lot of time together, but proximity alone doesn't make a relationship.

Never forget: you make God happy when you pray. Yes, even when you've just blown it. Especially when you've just blown it.

The second issue related to prayer we want to address is simply not knowing how. How do you pray about something that is such a big problem in your life? How do you pray about something you've tried again and again to correct, and failed every time? I (Joe) am something of an expert on this. I tell people to do what I do: go find a quiet place and just let out of your heart whatever is clawing to get out. Are you angry? Frustrated? Sad? Hurting? Sorry? Confused? Whatever you're feeling, open your mouth and let it fly. If that means yelling, yell. If it means weeping, weep. If it means griping or begging or even apologizing, do it. The last thing God wants from you is some sort of sterilized, cliché-laden, "Christian speak" prayer that doesn't come from your heart. Just be real. I promise, nothing that comes out of your mouth is going to surprise God.

We are a couple of guys who believe God answers prayer. John the apostle wrote, "And we are confident that he hears us whenever we ask for anything that pleases him. And since we know he hears us when we make our requests, we also know that he will give us what we ask for" (1 John 5:14-15). It makes no sense to attempt something as big as overcoming a besetting sin without getting serious about prayer. Without God, you can't succeed. With him, you can't fail.

Step Three: Prune

In the Sermon on the Mount, Jesus directly addressed the issue of besetting sins, and what he said has been causing people to break out in a cold sweat for two thousand years. Let's dig in and try to learn something. Jesus said:

> You have heard that it was said, 'Do not commit adultery.' But I tell you that anyone who looks at a woman to lust after her has already committed adultery with her in his heart. If your right eye causes you to sin, gouge it out and throw it away. It is better for you to lose one part of your body than for your whole body to be thrown into hell. And if your right hand causes you to sin, cut it off and throw it away. It is better for you to lose one of the parts of your body than for your whole body to go into hell. (Matthew 5:27–30 HCSB)

Yes, Jesus is using hyperbole here. If you slept through your high school English class, hyperbole is an obvious exaggeration for the purpose of making a point. Maybe you've said, "That engine purrs like a kitten" or that a basketball player can "jump out of the building." Such comments are ridiculous if taken literally, but they nail the truth if understood as hyperbole.

Make no mistake, these words of Jesus are hyperbole, and they absolutely nail the truth: There's no way you will ever conquer your besetting sin without some pruning. Prioritize and pray all you want. If you skip this step, you can kiss victory goodbye. Let's make sure we understand the implications of this teaching.

The first thing we want to point out is that, even though Jesus specifically mentions adultery here, the instruction he offers applies to any besetting sin. Some people have tried to excuse themselves from the hard truths in this passage by pointing out that they don't struggle with lust. Sorry, but that bird won't fly. This passage is for everyone with a nagging, persistent, besetting sin. Note three critical truths.

Critical Truth #1: The stakes are high.

Extremely high.

Twice in this passage, Jesus mentions that hell is one of the possible outcomes for a person in the grip of a besetting sin: "It is better for you to lose one part of your body than for your whole body to be thrown into hell." We love how brutally honest Jesus is. In the modern church there is a lot of soft preaching. The primary goal seems to be to send people out the door on Sunday feeling good about themselves, even if there's no reason why they should feel good about themselves. Not so with Jesus. He is full of grace and understanding, but that doesn't mean he won't be honest with you. While most of the world is downplaying sin or denying it altogether, or even renaming it with pretty words (don't get us started!), Jesus will always tell you the truth.

Critical Truth #2: Radical measures are necessary.

I (Mark) once knew a nurse who worked in the ER. Having visited hospitals and emergency rooms my entire adult life, I know how frantic, how bloody, and how touch-and-go things can be in that environment. One day I asked her, "Isn't your stress level off the charts? Wouldn't you prefer to work in some other area of the hospital?" I was fascinated by her answer. She said, "Absolutely not. The ER is where lives often hang in the balance. Sometimes we get patients who are minutes away from death. In that situation, every move I make matters. I never have to wonder if my life has a purpose."

She also talked about how surgery is often the difference between life and death. Some patients can be treated with a bandage or an IV, but for others cutting is the only answer. Jesus is clearly talking about people who have reached a similar point in their spiritual lives. He says, "If your right hand causes you to sin, cut it off and throw it away."

Your challenge is to take a hard look at your daily routine and figure out what needs to be cut out in order to save your life. We encourage you to look at three specific areas: habits, relationships, and technology.

Habits have a way of growing or deepening. A beer after dinner can turn into two or three or four or more. Checking your social media before bed can turn into two hours of scrolling while your mate sits (and feels) all alone. Even an innocent pastime like golf can turn into an every-weekend event with your buddies that costs you important time with your family.

Relationships, if they are unhealthy, can bring out the worst in us. Someone with a dirty mind can have you laughing at jokes and thinking erotic thoughts you'd be ashamed to share with any of your Christian friends. An attractive, flirtatious coworker can slowly draw you onto a path that could lead to an affair and the destruction of your reputation and your family. Someone with a negative, complaining spirit can turn you into an irritating sourpuss and make you as miserable as you make the people around you.

And then there's technology. For all the good it does, it may well do twice as much harm. It can pull you out of the real world and throw you into a garbage-dump universe that produces a steady stream of vulgar images, insipid podcasts, banal thirty-second videos, political bias, hate speech, and misinformation. Google "Is social media healthy?" and you will get close to three *billion* websites telling you it isn't.

While we're on the subject of technology, let's get real about pornography. Many of the people who read this chapter with great interest will have porn as their besetting sin. It's always been a problem for people, but when the Internet came along, it's like the world drove off a cliff. No longer did people have to seek out an old, seedy inner-city theater. Suddenly, porn could be indulged in the comforts of one's own home. Not to mention the fact that the Internet made porn available to children and minors.

We know you love your computer. We love ours too. But it's time we admitted that a computer can be a tremendous threat to your spiritual life and relationship with God. Even as you're holding this book and sliding your eyes across these words, you know in your heart if that is the case for you. If it is, read the next paragraph carefully.

If one or more of these things is keeping you locked in a bad place, you simply must do some cutting. The definition of insanity is to keep doing the same things over and over while believing you're eventually going to get a different result. Take it from two preachers who've talked to thousands of troubled people: the number one reason people are mired in their sin and can't get out is because they skip the pruning step. They judge it to be too painful. Or maybe deep down they don't really want to change. Whatever the reason, without the surgery Jesus describes, they're stuck in quicksand and destined to be swallowed up.

What are you going to do?

Critical Truth #3: Radical measures must be targeted.

Yes, radical measures are necessary, but they can't be overly broad or poorly aimed. To paraphrase Jesus, "If your right hand offends you, don't cut off your ear or your foot. Cut off that right hand." Far too many people who are struggling with sin overreact emotionally and start hacking and slashing things from their lives that have little bearing on their problem.

Back when we were in Bible college, it was fashionable for preachers and youth ministers to regale audiences about the evils of rock music. And yes, there was plenty of evil in the music of bands like Black Sabbath and Led Zeppelin. But time and time again, young people would race home from some youth conference, gather up all their albums and destroy them in a big bonfire, only to regret it sometime later when, in a moment of clarity, they realized they destroyed their perfectly harmless albums too. One man said, "I burned all my albums in a big youth group bonfire when I was seventeen. By the time I was twenty-five I had repurchased most of them because I realized there was nothing wrong with them."

That's exactly what we're talking about.

If alcohol is a temptation for you, don't raise your right hand and swear that you'll never go into a business that sells alcohol for the rest of your life. That's silly. Almost every restaurant and grocery store in America sells alcohol. You could starve to death! Instead, lay down some commonsense parameters, such as:

Never going to an establishment that serves *primarily* alcohol.

Never going *alone* to an establishment that sells alcohol.

Never going *with someone who drinks* to an establishment that sells alcohol.

There is always a sweet spot in situations like this, that place where you're doing what's necessary to solve the problem but not going overboard. Far too many people, instead of plucking out an eye or cutting off a hand as Jesus instructed, would pluck out both eyes and cut off both hands just to be on the safe side. The danger of going overboard is you create a life for yourself that you come to hate. You put yourself in such a tight box that you can't do anything or go anywhere without violating your unreasonable standards. And when you come to hate your life, that's when you're likely to plunge back into your old life like an Olympic high diver.

Critical Truth #4: Disposal is important.

Notice Jesus said to cut off your hand and "throw it away." Or pluck out your eye and "throw it away." To be able to throw it away, you have to cut all the way through. Far too many people cut alright, but they don't cut all the way through and dispose of the offending object. An example would be the guy who says to the woman he's in an inappropriate relationship with, "We can't keep doing this. We need to stop and just be friends."

Whoa, Nellie!

Stop and just be *friends*?

That, dear reader, is a cut that can be sewed back together very easily. When you make a statement like that, you're admitting that you don't want to really end the relationship, just tone it down a little. Which is the same as saying, "We're going to pretend this is over, but it really isn't."

We don't think it's an accident that Jesus spoke of throwing away the offending object. He's making sure we understand that half-measures won't cut it (pun intended) when it comes to a besetting sin.

Once again, pruning is the scary step people don't like and try to work around. Our guess is that ninety-nine percent of the people who fail in their efforts to overcome their besetting sin fail in this area. I (Joe) love John Owen's great statement: "Be killing sin, or sin will be killing you."

Step Four: Produce

When you cut something major out of your life, there will be a void left behind. However much time you spent thinking about your sin and indulging in it, all of it will suddenly be left empty. If you don't fill it with something, you'll likely fall right back into your old ways. You could find a new hobby or join a club or start taking piano lessons, but we believe Jesus would say you need to fill that void with something that will produce fruit for the Kingdom. When the disciples were in the upper room celebrating Passover, Jesus said to them, "When you produce much fruit, you are my true disciples. This brings great glory to my Father" (John 15:8).

The reason this is important is because fruit-bearing for the Kingdom focuses your mind and your life in a positive direction, which is critically important when you're trying to make profound changes. Piano lessons are great, but they're neutral, spiritually. When you're trying to defeat a besetting sin, you don't need neutral; you need spiritual. I (Joe) once heard a preacher say, "When God delivers you from an addiction, get as far away from that behavior and lifestyle as you can. Prisoners don't continue to hang around the prison after they are released." Some kind of fruit-bearing endeavor will help you get away from the prison.

If you can't think of any fruit-bearing endeavors, talk to your preacher and tell him you'd like to volunteer and serve in some area where there's a need. When he comes to after passing out, he will be glad to get you set up. But remember also that you can bear fruit outside the walls of the church. Befriend a shut-in, volunteer at a homeless shelter, or deliver meals on wheels. Anything that affords you an opportunity to serve and touch people's lives will be a big help to them and you.

Step Five: Persevere

We said earlier that the unwillingness to prune is probably the number one reason why so many people fail to conquer their besetting sin. Want to know what the number two reason is? Giving up too soon.

Far too many people, when they suffer a setback or have a weak moment or a bad day, go right back into "I can't" mode: "Looks like this stuff I've been doing isn't going to work after all. I guess I'm just too weak." You can bet that Satan, the accuser of the brethren, will be feeding and nourishing such thoughts like a lawn guy spreading fertilizer.[12] The one thing he won't want you to do is hang in there and try again. Why? Because he knows the power of perseverance.

One of my (Joe's) favorite sports stories is Kurt Warner's journey to NFL royalty and the Hall of Fame. In 1994, he was bagging groceries for $5.50 an hour after being cut by the Green Bay Packers. Believing in spite of all available evidence that he could play and excel as a professional quarterback, he decided to give the Arena Football League a try. Granted, it wasn't the NFL, but he knew that NFL scouts kept an eye on the league, and that if he could play well, it might lead to another shot.

He did and it did.

Just five years later, in his first season with the St. Louis Rams, Kurt Warner won the league MVP, the Super Bowl, and the Super Bowl MVP. He went from making $5.50 an hour to signing a deal for $47 million and was inducted into the NFL Hall of Fame in 2017.

It doesn't matter if you're talking about football or spiritual growth, the power of perseverance is often the difference-maker. Read about any successful historical figure, from King David to Abraham Lincoln, and

---

[12] Revelation 12:10

you'll see multiple failures in his or her backstory. The only reason we know their names today is because they didn't quit when things were tough.

The author of the book of Hebrews exhorted his readers to "run with endurance the race God has set before us" (Hebrews 12:1). That is our closing exhortation to you. Conquering your besetting sin is very doable. With God's help and some good decision-making, you *can* do it!

6

Yes, You *Can* Live Righteously in a Cesspool

*Anyone who does not live righteously...
cannot belong to God.*
1 John 3:10

YOU'VE HEARD THE OLD saying, "It's not always what you do, but what you *don't* do that gets you into trouble."

I (Joe), am exhibit A.

About ten years ago, I failed to make a simple phone call. The call would have taken no more than two minutes. It would have had no stress whatsoever attached to it. I could have hung up the phone and gone on happily with my day. But because I failed to make the call, my family and I suffered terribly. You see, I forgot to call and have the septic tank pumped out.

There are a lot of things you can fail to do as a homeowner, and life will go on just fine: paint, power wash the driveway, clean out your garage, etc. But if you fail to call the septic tank people, eventually it will be like one of the plagues of Egypt is being visited on your home. The filthiest, nastiest gunk you can imagine will start backing up into your house. And your family members, knowing you were the guy who was supposed to make the call, will start contemplating whether they should let you live.

In my defense, as soon as I got a whiff (literally) of the trouble I had caused, I dropped everything and began working on the problem. I made the call. I drove all over town buying every jug of bleach I could find. I mopped and cleaned and disinfected and begged my family to let me go on living with them.

Let's just say I know a little something about cesspools.

Our culture has become a cesspool.

We don't know a sane person who would dispute this. Even people who don't love God—people who don't even care about spiritual things—will agree that, morally, our country is rapidly spiraling downward. We could quote enough stats about crime and addiction and pornography and sexual deviancy to keep you reading for an hour. But we won't because we know we don't need to convince you. You're not blind. You see it all around you. You know things are worse—much worse—than they used to be. For crying out loud, there are now drag queens and strippers performing in elementary schools! (Those are some words we never thought we'd write.)

Here's the problem: God has called us to live righteously in this cesspool: "So put to death the sinful, earthly things lurking within you. Have nothing to do with sexual immorality, impurity, lust, and evil desires" (Colossians 3:5).

Most Christians wish Paul had stuck the word *try* in there.

"*Try* to put to death the sinful earthly things."

"*Try* to have nothing to do with sexual immorality."

That he didn't makes the commands seem out of reach. Many people say, "Wait a minute, Paul. You're being unreasonable. It sounds like you're asking us to live and work in a sewer wearing a white dress or tuxedo without getting any stains on our clothes. We can't do that! It's impossible!"

We want to be clear: Paul is not demanding perfection. There's no such thing in this world, and God would not ask us to do the impossible. But he is calling us to live righteously.

What does that mean?

Very simply, righteous living is the exceptional attitude and behavior a person exhibits when his or her heart is fully inclined toward God.

Again, note: not perfect, but exceptional.

It's a life that is noticeably different, the kind of life Jesus was talking about when he told his followers they were the light of the world, shining in the darkness (Matthew 5:16). You know people like this. People whose appearance and demeanor and speech and life choices set them apart from the masses. A cynic would derisively call them extreme or fanatical. Or maybe a stick in the mud. Yet even that cynic, if he were stranded on a deserted highway at night and saw a car slowing down to stop, would hope and pray that such a person was behind the wheel.

But we're not going to sugarcoat anything. Living this way is hard. Real hard. We can think of four factors that make righteous living a challenge.

One is the *weakness of the flesh*. Jesus said to his disciples, "Keep watch and pray, so that you will not give in to temptation. For the spirit is willing, but the body is weak" (Matthew 26:41). Every person alive has a weakness or two or ten. Every day millions of dieters sneak a Big Mac at lunch or hide chocolate candy in their desks at work. Millions of shoppers buy clothing or shoes they don't need. Millions of husbands and wives flirt with someone other than their spouse. Right now, without even taking a minute to think, you could probably itemize some of your own weaknesses. You could probably also think of a few instances when they got you into trouble. Maybe more than a few.

A second factor that makes righteous living a challenge is *peer pressure*. Proverbs says, "Don't do as the wicked do, and don't follow the path of evildoers. Don't even think about it; don't go that way" (Proverbs 4:14–15). The problem is, the wicked are constantly enticing you—even pressuring you—to follow their path. And they can be very persuasive. Their lives can seem so interesting and fun and make you feel boring by comparison. Especially if they have more friends than you do, or more money. And, in many cases, they don't seem to be suffering at all for their choices. It all can look very appealing.

In fact, Peter explains that your former friends will be "surprised when you no longer plunge into the flood of the wild and destructive things they do" (1 Peter 4:4). When he talks about the flood of the wild and destructive things they do, he's imagining a cesspool. Like what backs up into your house when you don't call the septic tank people. The point is that the wicked are so used to peer pressure working that they are surprised when it doesn't.

A third factor that makes righteous living a challenge is *discouragement*. Remember Elijah? He was a dynamo for God until he learned that the evil Queen Jezebel had put a price on his head and sent her hit men after him. That news so discouraged him that he literally gave up and asked God to kill him (1 Kings 19:1–4). Being discouraged puts a hole in your bucket of "want to." You begin to think, "What's the point? Why should I waste my time trying? It's all a waste." Maybe you had this very thought flash through your mind in the past when you were struggling to break a bad habit, and then promptly fell off the wagon.

And a fourth factor that makes righteous living a challenge is *desensitization*. We grew up in a generation when television was tasteful. Rob and Laura Petrie slept in separate beds on the Dick Van Dyke Show. About the raciest thing we saw on TV as kids was Ginger slinking around in her sequined dress on *Gilligan's Island*, or maybe Gomez Addams kissing his way up Morticia's arm on *The Addams Family*. Compare that to today, when nudity and violence and profanity are the norm. If the change had happened overnight, we all would have had coronaries. But because it happened little by little, we slowly became desensitized. Now, we see Christians posting on social media about how much they love the vilest shows on television, like *Game of Thrones*. They are so desensitized that it doesn't even occur to them to be ashamed or embarrassed.

Are any or all of these four factors keeping you from living righteously? If someone were to follow you around all week without your knowledge and watch everything you do, would they come away impressed with your level of purity and wholesomeness, or would they be surprised, even shocked, at the things you do?

We're going to assume you're a serious Christian. We don't think you'd pick up a book like this and read it if you weren't. And if you are a serious Christian, we assume you want to live righteously to honor the God who saved you and put forth the best possible witness. Further, we assume righteous living is hard for you (like it is for us), and perhaps even seems impossible at times. With those assumptions in mind, we want to share our thoughts on some pretty admirable qualities and strategies that seem like they would guarantee righteousness but don't.

The Pursuit of Righteousness: What Doesn't Work

Self-Discipline

We are big fans of self-discipline. It's what keeps most people from saying every rude thing that pops into their head, from showing up an hour or two late for work every day, and from eating junk food for every meal. It's what motivates students to do their homework, athletes to stay in shape, and musicians to practice. We can tell you firsthand that it's what enables books to be written. Oh yes, we are big fans of self-discipline. But we are forced to admit that self-discipline doesn't guarantee righteousness. Why? Because it's so fluctuating. It ebbs and flows with our moods and circumstances.

King David is a good example. He was a man after God's own heart, but one day he was in a mood as he strolled around on the palace roof. When he looked across the way and saw the beautiful Bathsheba bathing, every shred of self-discipline he had melted away like snow on the Fourth of July, and the next thing you know, they were in bed together.

This is the problem with self-discipline: it is very susceptible to weak moments.

And we all have weak moments.

I (Joe) once got thrown out of a Bible college basketball game. No, I wasn't playing. I was the bus driver for the team. But sitting there watching those blind officials making bad call after bad call, I lost it. Do you understand how hard it is to get thrown out of a basketball game when you're just the bus driver? It's practically impossible! But I accomplished the feat in an epic moment of weakness.

Unfortunately, sometimes moments of weakness turn into much more than moments. They can get dragged out to encompass a much longer period of time. David's moment of weakness turned into what some scholars say was a *year* of weakness as he maneuvered and manipulated circumstances to have Bathsheba's husband killed so he could take her as his wife (2 Samuel 11).

There's also the matter of frequency. If you have only a moment of weakness once every five years, we'll just call you righteous, and you can skip ahead to the next chapter. But if like most people, your moments of weakness are more frequent, maybe not. Some people have multiple weak moments every day.

Again, we are very pro-self-discipline. We wish more people had more of it. We wish *we* had more of it! But self-discipline is no guarantee of sustained righteousness. How many people do you suppose are sitting in jail cells at this moment because their self-discipline went bye-bye in a moment of weakness? How many marriages have been mortally wounded by a moment of weakness? How many ministries? Millions of broken people have asked, "Where was my self-discipline when I needed it?"

Separation

Separation from the things of the world as a strategy for righteousness is not new. About five hundred years after Christ, Benedict of Nursia decided to live as a hermit in order to achieve greater holiness. When others wanted to join him, he set up a communal residence and thus became known as the father of Western monasticism. Benedictine monks made three vows: poverty, chastity, and obedience.

Seems like a great idea, doesn't it? If you don't want to be tempted by the things of this world, just separate yourself from them. What could be simpler?

Here's our question: Why do people think Satan can't show up in a monastery?

In fact, why does anyone think Satan wouldn't look at a monastery or a convent and lick his chops? Why wouldn't he take special delight in getting in there and planting thoughts of envy, jealousy, and resentment in the hearts of those people who have sequestered themselves from the pleasures of the world? Maybe they're not having drunken parties, but do we really believe there is a place on this earth where Satan can't wield his influence?

But let's forget monasteries and convents and think about the way most people today try to separate themselves from the things of this world. They don't go to the movies or watch TV or read secular books or hang out with or even work with unbelievers. We both have known unemployed people who passed up opportunities for good jobs because they were holding out for a job where they would be working for and with only Christians.

This bothers us on a couple of levels.

First, if the goal really is to be like Jesus, we have to remember that he hung out with sinners. He was even called a friend of sinners (Matthew 11:19, Luke 7:34). No, he didn't condone or participate in their lifestyle, but he certainly did engage them in conversations and try to influence them. Levi, a tax collector who became Matthew, one of Jesus's disciples and the writer of the first book of the New Testament, is an example of the fruit that was borne by Jesus's willingness to mix and mingle with "undesirable" people.

Also, we've been called by Jesus to be salt and light in the world (Matthew 5:13–16). How are we supposed to accomplish that if we never interact with unbelievers? In fact, if Jesus called us to "go into all the world" and make disciples, and we choose to hang out only with believers and never engage the lost, isn't that in itself a sin? Aren't we disobeying Jesus's command? And wouldn't that disobedience go a long way toward negating the righteousness we think we're achieving by separating ourselves from the world?

To be clear: we're not saying you shouldn't separate yourself from some things—and even some people—who are a bad influence on you. But to think you can achieve righteousness by completely disengaging with the world is nonsense. Jesus wants us to be *in* the world, just not *of* the world (John 17:15).

Saturation

"Idle hands are the devil's playground." You've probably heard that old saying, which is a backhanded endorsement of busyness as a way to keep the devil at bay. Saturate your life with as many activities as possible so you don't have time to get into trouble. And we do not deny that there is some value in staying busy, as opposed to having lots of free time. The problem is that busyness opens doors to the devil too.

Stress is the most obvious problem that comes from having your life packed with wall-to-wall activities. You might be able to keep all the plates spinning for a while, but eventually they will start wobbling and you will be running back and forth, increasingly desperate to keep them from crashing. And when one does crash, Satan will be right there to condemn you for failing. We've counseled countless people who felt like failures for not being able to keep all their plates spinning, when they never should have allowed themselves to become so busy in the first place.

A second problem that arises when you fill your life to the brim with activity is that quality suffers. You're doing so much that you don't really do anything well. Your life becomes an exercise in mediocrity. In particular, your marriage and your parenting can become mediocre because you're not devoting adequate time to your spouse and kids. Probably your spiritual life will be suffering too as you find yourself too busy to devote time to the spiritual disciplines.

So maybe you solve one problem by filling your life with activity, but you create others by being too busy. It's like a baseball team that needs offense. They trade some pitchers away to get some good hitters, only to discover that while their hitting is much better their pitching stinks, and they're still a bad team.

Seriousness

When all else fails in the pursuit of righteousness, you can just knuckle down and get super-serious about it. Put on your game face and quit fooling around. Sit up straight and put your feet flat on the floor. Wipe that smile off your face. Suck in that gut. No more frivolity. No more listening to music that isn't Christian. No more movies. No more playing softball with your beer-drinking coworkers in the city rec league. And as for those Seinfeld reruns, no siree Bob! From now on there will be no enjoyment of life as long as there are Scriptures to study and prayers to utter.

Obviously, we wrote that last paragraph with our tongues firmly planted in our cheeks.

Or did we?

We have actually known people who took this approach to the pursuit of righteousness. You probably have too. We know Jesus encountered people like this; they were called Pharisees. Talk about serious. Mr. Rogers would look like a vaudeville comedian compared to those guys. They were so serious about their religion that they actually made up more rules to follow because they felt God didn't give them enough. Now *that's* serious!

The thing is, of all the people Jesus ever met, he condemned them more than anybody else. Which tells us that seriousness is no measure of righteousness. If it were, they would have been the all-time righteousness champs. Not that seriousness can't be a good thing in moderation, it just doesn't make you righteous. It could, however, make you judgmental and legalistic toward people who aren't as serious as you. That was the problem with the Pharisees. What they thought elevated them spiritually actually diminished them.

Millions of people pursue righteousness in the ways we've just listed and wonder why they make little, if any, progress. They put honest effort into it with high hopes and then feel defeated when nothing really changes. They still trip over the same old stumbling blocks. They still experience the same failures they were sure they would overcome. Eventually, they become convinced that they just can't live righteously in a cesspool.

But they're wrong!

The Pursuit of Righteousness: What Does Work

As we see it, the best way to achieve righteousness is through surrender. *Surrender* is a word you won't hear too often in the modern church. We can't even remember the last time we heard that great old hymn

"I Surrender All." We hear a lot about fighting the good fight and resisting the devil and fleeing from sin and all kinds of other action-oriented strategies, all of which are very good and biblical. But you almost never hear anyone talk about surrendering. We think surrender is one of the most overlooked and under-appreciated doctrines in Scripture.

We have a couple of theories as to why that is.

In his letter to the Philippians, Paul writes about how Jesus gave up his perfect existence in heaven and came to earth to live as a man and to suffer, even to the point of death on a cross. At the end of the passage, Paul writes that "at the name of Jesus every knee should bow, in heaven and on earth and under the earth, and every tongue confess that Jesus Christ is Lord to the glory of God the Father"(Philippians 2:10–11). That's some serious surrender right there. But we Christians tend to think of the future when we read these words. We understand Paul to be saying that *someday* every knee will bow. *Someday* every tongue will confess. *Someday* there will be complete surrender to the Lordship of Christ. Does this cause us not to think of surrender as a here-and-now thing?

Or maybe it's the title King of kings and Lord of lord's we don't connect with. It's used in the Bible in reference to Jesus numerous times, but we Americans aren't accustomed to kings. We have presidents, which are often not trusted or even respected by millions of people. Our national leaders are some of the most unpopular people in America. We criticize them, ridicule them, make jokes about them, and impeach them. You don't do any of that with a king. Instead, you humbly bow. You surrender yourself to his service. You've seen a hundred movies where the king's knights or servants or even the assembled masses drop to one knee and bow before the royal monarch. Perhaps this is why we'd rather think of Jesus as a friend or a savior than a king. That bowing business just seems so . . . medieval.

Yet, according to Jesus himself, it's surrender that is the key to following him. Read carefully his words to a crowd of potential followers:

> If any of you wants to be my follower, you must give up your own way, take up your cross, and follow me. If you try to hang onto your life, you will lose it. But if you give up your life for my sake, and for the sake of the Good News, you will save it. (Mark 8:34–35)

These words are telling. He doesn't warn them that they're going to have to fight really hard if they want to become his followers. He doesn't tell them to buckle their chin straps and get ready for a rumble with the devil's forces to prove themselves. No, he tells them to give up their lives for his sake. That's as clear a picture of surrender as there could ever be. We believe a lot of Christians struggle with righteousness because they skipped this essential step in God's plan for them. Yes, they acknowledged Jesus as their Savior and submitted to baptism, but they didn't bow before him as Lord. They didn't truly give up their lives for his sake.

Christians today like to say, "I made a commitment to Christ." Here's what we have to understand: Surrender and commitment are not the same thing.

Commitment is something that fluctuates according to our moods or circumstances. Earlier, we mentioned King David's sin with Bathsheba. If you had asked him before he spotted Bathsheba if he was committed to God, he would have said yes. But in that critical moment his commitment was diluted by the mood he was in and likely by the fact that he was alone. He was susceptible to temptation. And so, when he saw Bathsheba bathing, his resolve was nowhere to be found.

Maybe you've experienced this with a diet. Some days you're really strong and no slice of chocolate cake in the world could shake your resolve. But on other days you would smash your face into that piece of cake like a one-year-old at his birthday party. This is why people lose weight and then gain it back repeatedly throughout their lives. Commitment fluctuates.

Or maybe you experienced this truth in your marriage. When you stood before the preacher on your wedding day, you were one thousand percent committed. You were marrying for life, period, end of story. But just a couple of years later you were sitting in front of a marriage counselor trying to decide if you even loved the person you married. Or if he (or she) was even human. Commitment fluctuates.

Which brings us back to surrender.

Surrender is not many decisions you make throughout your life. It is one decision—a one-and-done choice you make that determines the entire direction of your life going forward. It is not dependent on moods or circumstances. And it has no trial period with a money-back guarantee if it turns out you don't like it. Going in with an opt-out clause isn't surrender. Just sticking your toe into the water to gauge the temperature isn't surrender. Surrender is diving in headfirst and never looking back.

There are many beautiful pictures of surrender in the Bible. One of our favorites is Shadrach, Meshack, and Abednego in Daniel 3. We love how they didn't huddle up to discuss the pros and cons of choosing God over Nebuchadnezzar, even when Nebuchadnezzar threatened to throw them into blazing hot furnace if they did. There was no need for a discussion because their decision had been made long ago. They were going to be faithful no matter what the consequences were. That's surrender.

In the New Testament, Peter and John are a great example of surrender. When the Jewish leaders threw them in jail and threatened them with bodily harm if they didn't shut up about Jesus, they didn't ask for a recess to discuss the situation. Their decision had been made long ago. They simply said, "Do you think God wants us to obey you rather than him? We cannot stop telling about everything we have seen and heard" (Acts 4:19–20).

Commitment is good; surrender is better.

Here are three facts about surrendering to the Lord that may help you further.

Fact #1: Surrender to the Lord is unconditional.

We're accustomed to hearing about terms of surrender being negotiated. That's not how it works with Christians. We don't come to God with a proposal that seems fair to both sides. We don't say, "Lord, if you'll cut me some slack on tithing, I promise to work extra hard around the church building when repairs are needed." There are actually people who think this way. We've met hundreds of them! You'll hear them say things like this: "I don't give money to the church. I consider my service to be my tithe because, after all, time is money."

Nope. Nope. Nope. That's not surrender.

When Jesus told people to give up their lives for his sake, he meant *all* of their lives.

Fact #2: Surrender is forward looking.

Surrender is about leaving behind the things in our lives that keep us from God. Far too many people want to hang onto this or that questionable activity or habit, thinking that one little indulgence is no big deal if it doesn't hurt anybody. But God expects us to leave all that stuff behind. Remember when Lot's family fled Sodom? An angel told them not to look back as they fled the coming destruction (Genesis 19:17). There was nothing back there they needed. Nothing that would help them in any way moving forward. But Lot's wife wasn't so sure, and she looked back. She may have been walking toward the city limits, but she wasn't fully surrendered. And God turned her into a pillar of salt.

Fact #3: Surrender is positive.

In 2022, Josh Duncan built an eight-foot wooden cross, attached a wheel to it, and wheeled it four miles every day along a busy highway near his home. Even though we're pretty sure the cross Jesus carried didn't have a wheel attached to it, we'll not judge Josh on his choice to add one. We will, however, point out that in the New Testament Christians didn't win favor among the unsaved masses by lugging wooden crosses around with agonized expressions on their faces. They did it by lovingly sharing and ministering to each other: "There were no needy people among them, because those who owned land or houses would sell them and bring the money to the apostles to give to those in need" (Acts 4:34). Not to mention the fact that the apostles were busy healing people (Acts 5:12). Mark it down: the spirit of true surrender is always winsome and positive. The early church was threatened and persecuted. Believers were martyred right and left. Still, our earliest brothers and sisters put forth an overwhelmingly positive, upbeat, joyful witness that expressed itself in kindness and drew thousands into their fellowship. If you meet someone today who claims to be surrendered to the Lord but doesn't seem happy about it, something's wrong.

We have been singing the praises of surrender as the best way to live a righteous life in the cesspool that is our culture. We actually think it's the only way. We want to close by pointing you to an obscure passage of Scripture in Exodus 21.

In ancient Israel, a poor Jew could actually sell himself into slavery as a way of paying his debts. If he did this, he would only be obligated to serve his master for six years. However, if at the end of that six-year period, he had come to love his master and knew that he would have a better life if he remained a slave and continued to live under his master's authority, he could make that choice. But if he did so, it would be permanent (Exodus 21:2-6).

This is essentially the choice we Christians have to make. Do we want to go our own way, or do we want to surrender *permanently* to the authority of our Master, Jesus? There is no halfway meeting in the middle, no compromise. A half-surrendered Christian is not a surrendered Christian. We either have to surrender completely or not at all.

If we do surrender completely, our lives will show it. We won't be perfect, but we absolutely will appear as lights in the darkness.

Or as diamonds in the cesspool.

7

Yes, You *Can* Live Guilt-Free with a Long Rap Sheet

*So now there is no condemnation for those
who belong to Christ Jesus.*
Romans 8:1

YOU'VE PROBABLY WATCHED ENOUGH movies to know what a RAP sheet is. Officially, it stands for Record of Arrests and Prosecutions. As we put this chapter together, we found ourselves wondering who had the longest RAP sheet of all time. A few Google searches led us to a former investigator who claims to have known of a thirty-five-year-old man who had one that was fifteen feet long. It included over one hundred arrests and prosecutions, including eleven DUI and drug charges. It wasn't until he robbed a bank that they finally put him away.

To be clear, we're not suggesting that you have a literal RAP sheet, though you might. We're using the idea of a RAP sheet metaphorically, to refer to the things you've done in your life that you look back on with horror and shame. They may not have been illegal. In fact, they may have been celebrated by the people you were with at the time. But now that you are older and wiser, and perhaps with different values, you cringe when you think about what you did. And perhaps weep.

Just two weeks before we started work on this chapter, a terrible tragedy happened just about a mile from my (Mark) house. Two grandparents were taking their grandkids home after a Sunday evening outing. On a residential street just two blocks from their destination, they were T-boned by a fifteen-year-old driver who blew through an intersection going seventy miles per hour. The grandmother, age fifty-one, was killed instantly, along with all three grandchildren, ages eleven, eight, and one. The grandfather made it to the hospital, clinging to life. The driver survived.

There's so much to think about in a situation like that. So much that is heartbreaking. The loss is unimaginable, the questions without end. But sooner or later your thoughts come around to that fifteen-year-old driver, and one question looms above all others: How do you live with something like that?

That's what this chapter is about.

We've all sinned and fallen short of the glory of God (Romans 3:23). But let's face it: some of our sins don't keep us awake nights. I (Mark) got a few raps on my posterior with a paddle when I was in the sixth grade (yes, teachers could spank in those days) because I used a rubber band to shoot a straw at a female classmate who got on my nerves. Just as I let the straw fly (it hit her in the arm), the teacher walked into the room. Busted! Out of the room I marched, down the hall to the principal's office, like a condemned man to the gallows. The only things missing were handcuffs and an orange jumpsuit. (I later discovered through pats on the back and numerous attaboys that I was a hero to the other boys in the class who also found the girl exceedingly annoying.)

That's not the kind of sin we're talking about here.

King David could explain the kind of sin we're talking about. After his affair with Bathsheba and his murderous plot against her husband, he wrote that his guilt haunted him "day and night" (Psalm 51:3). He would have agreed with the Roman playwright Seneca, who observed that a guilty person is his own hangman.

There are at least three reasons why guilt is so painful.

One is that time only moves forward. As much as you may wish you could, you can't go back and fix anything. How many times have you said, "If only I could do that over again." But you can't. What's done is done. Perhaps this is why people have always been drawn to time-travel stories. That longing to be able to go back and fix things is very powerful.

Two is because Satan is an accuser and simply will not let you forget (Revelation 12:10). Every time you turn around, he'll be throwing your sin in your face. And something else: he will embellish and exaggerate. He'll try to get you to believe you're the most despicable human being who ever lived, or that God is disgusted with you and wants nothing to do with you.

And three is because of the grudges people hold. You hear about the awful things the people you hurt say about you. If you encounter them, you can see the hate in their eyes and feel the animosity radiating off of them. They may even threaten you or even worse.

We want to pause right here and comment on the hatred others may have for you because of your sin. The apostle Paul told the Christians in Rome to "do all that you can to live in peace with everyone" (Romans 12:18). Some versions say, "As far as it depends on you live at peace with everyone" (NIV). The message is clear: there are people you will never be able to make peace with. They are going to hate you until their dying breath. Your job is to try to make peace but not to worry about it if you give it your best shot and can't. Remember, those people aren't going to have a vote on where you spend eternity when you stand before God.

The point is guilt is a beast. The English poet Nicholas Rowe was spot on when he wrote that guilt is like an avenging fiend that follows along behind you with a whip. According to our experience as pastors, there are a lot of avenging fiends with whips out there.

A few years ago, Tomoka Christian Church conducted an anonymous survey of our people, and I (Joe) was struck by the results. One of the questions we asked was *What are you struggling with?* The darkness in the answers we got was unsettling, but not really surprising:

"I have an STD."

"I'm having an affair."
"I can't stop stealing."
"I am addicted to porn."
"I had a homosexual experience."
And on and on and on.

Reading the surveys was heartbreaking. You could almost feel the pain radiating from the paper. It was sobering for me as the people's pastor because I knew it was my responsibility to help them. Climbing Mt. Everest barefooted seemed like it might be an easier assignment.

Conviction or Guilt?

Anytime the subject of guilt comes up, it's important to make sure everyone understands the difference between the conviction that comes from the Holy Spirit and pure guilt. Both are extremely painful and therefore might be difficult to tell apart. But they are not the same thing.

When Jesus told his disciples that the Holy Spirit was coming, he made it clear that part of his work would be to convict people of their sin (John 16:8). This is a wonderful thing, for without the conviction of our sin, we would feel no need for Christ. And yes, the conviction of sin can be extremely painful. When Peter betrayed Jesus, he wept like the broken man he was in that moment (Luke 22:54–62).

But Peter wasn't the only disciple who betrayed Jesus; Judas did too (Matthew 26:47–49). The difference was not in their actions or the terrible feeling that overwhelmed them afterward. The difference was in the way they responded to that feeling. Peter went on to become an apostle and one of the great leaders of the early church while Judas hung himself. Clearly, Peter was being influenced by God, and Judas was being influenced by Satan. Peter was being nudged toward redemption, and Judas was being nudged toward death. In the simplest terms, this is the difference between the conviction of the Holy Spirit and the guilt trip Satan lays on us. Paul even said, "For the kind of sorrow God wants us to experience leads us away from sin and results in salvation" (2 Corinthians 7:10).

Right now, if something you've done has left a sick feeling in your gut, be very careful. Any impulses you have that would lead you to give up or harm yourself are from Satan. Satan will absolutely pull out that word *can't* and fire it at you like bullets from a machine gun:

"You know you can't beat this sin. It owns you!"

"You know you can't repair the damage. What's done is done."

"You know you can't go to heaven. Heaven is for *good* people not trash like you."

Our purpose in this chapter is to steer you away from Satan's can'ts and show you the biblical answer for a long and painful rap sheet.

The Amazing Grace of God

We've talked to a lot of believers who were struggling under a load of guilt, and we can assure you that their biggest worry is not about what they did or how they feel about what they did. Their biggest worry is about God's grace. They want to know if it's big and wide and deep enough to cover what they did.

Many of the great hymns of the faith assure us that it is. The great eighteenth-century English hymn writer William Cowper wrote:

> There is a fountain filled with blood
> Drawn from Immanuel's veins;
> And sinners, plunged beneath that flood,
> Lose all their guilty stains.

Not some, *all.*

Or this one:

> Would you be free from your burden of sin?
> There's power in the blood, power in the blood![13]

Or the granddaddy of all hymns of forgiveness:

> Amazing grace, how sweet the sound
> That saved a wretch like me.
> I once was lost, but now I'm found,
> 'twas blind, but now I see.[14]

---

[13] Lewis E. Jones, "Power in the Blood," written in 1899.
[14] John Newton, "Amazing Grace," written in 1772.

We both grew up singing these hymns, as did many of the people who will read this book. Often, there would be two, three, maybe even four songs in one Sunday service that would reference the sufficiency of God's grace. But here's what we know: singing encouraging hymns is nice, but when guilt drops on you like an anvil from a ten-story building, you're going to need more than the words of a gifted poet or the sweet notes of a talented musician; you're going to need the words of God himself:

> When we were utterly helpless, Christ came at just the right time and died for us sinners. Now, most people would not be willing to die for an upright person, though someone might perhaps be willing to die for a person who is especially good. But God showed his great love for us by sending Christ to die for us while we were still sinners. And since we have been made right in God's sight by the blood of Christ, he will certainly save us from God's condemnation. For since our friendship with God was restored by the death of his Son while we were still his enemies, we will certainly be saved through the life of his Son. So now we can rejoice in our wonderful new relationship with God because our Lord Jesus Christ has made us friends of God. (Romans 5:6–11)

There are four life-giving facts in this passage for anyone with a long RAP sheet.

Life-Giving Fact #1: God is not put off by our sin.

Time and time again throughout our lives, we reject people we don't approve of. I'll never forget the day my (Mark) wife, Marilyn, and I went car shopping. We had done some online research but wanted to test drive a particular car, so we drove to the nearest dealership. The salesman who approached us apparently gave no thought to the possibility that we might be Christians. Right out of the gate he used profanity and even made a couple of off-color comments that were supposed to be funny but to us only made him seem creepy. We felt uncomfortable the whole time we talked with him. When we left, we both agreed that we wouldn't buy a car from that guy if he were the last salesman on earth.

Have you ever had an experience like that?

If so, you know the feeling of being put off by other people's bad behavior. And don't you feel some level of pride when it happens? Don't you feel kind of good about yourself as if your disgust is a confirmation of your status as a good human being? Maybe you've even said, "I'm not putting up with that. I don't deserve to be talked to that way. I'm outta here!"

It's experiences like this that cause us trouble when *we* are the ones who have behaved badly. We naturally assume that God feels the way we would. How could he not? He is holy and we are pathetic. His righteousness is spotless and without blemish while ours is like filthy rags. We can't imagine him not being disgusted by us.

But he isn't.

We love how this passage explains the magnitude of God's love and grace by pointing out that, while we were still sinners, Christ died for us. This means that, far from being repulsed and pulling away from us, God actually leaned in.

Dear readers, that's huge! What a difference it makes to know that God is not put off by our sin. In fact, when we are at our worst, God is at his best. Yes, he might let us suffer the consequences of our sin as a way of teaching us, but he won't abandon us. You might be surprised to know that, even when you're neck deep in sin and failure, God is poised, just waiting for a sign of repentance from you so he can fly into action.

Think about Samson.

I (Mark) wrote a book about the Bible's strongest man, who was also the weakest. He could bench press chariots, but he couldn't resist the curves of a woman's body. The guy was the Hugh Hefner of his day, the playboy of playboys, a reality made doubly tragic by the fact that God had placed a high calling on his life: to lead his people, the Israelites, out of bondage to the Philistines. Samson, a man who could legitimately be said to have possessed the greatest potential of any Bible character, frittered it all away by chasing women. He chose to lay his head on the lap of the gorgeous Delilah and let her feed him grapes rather than doing what God called him to do. And yes, God let him suffer for his choices. His eyes were gouged out and he was imprisoned (Judges 16:21).

But God never abandoned him.

Even when he was a pitiful wreck of a man, God heard his prayer, his request to strengthen him one more time so he could push down the pillars of the temple and strike a major blow against the Philistines.

It wasn't even a perfect prayer. It contained no apology for his squandered life, and it seemed to be inspired by his desire for revenge (v. 28). Still, God heard and answered the prayer, which proves that God was right there, waiting and watching and listening for even the smallest sign of a positive turn in Samson's heart.

The simple truth is this: God doesn't abandon sinners.

He hates our sin. He is hurt by our sin. But he doesn't recoil from it. You may run from him, but he won't run from you. Why? Because he isn't willing for any to perish (2 Peter 3:9).

Life-Giving Fact #2: God's grace saves us from condemnation.

I (Joe) feel heartbroken every time I think about a close friend of mine. He had a very high rank in the military and was active in our church. After he left the service, he went to work for the FBI. I will never know what happened, or why, but one day he committed suicide. When I heard the news, I was stunned. But not half as stunned as I was when I learned more of the details. You see, he left behind a suicide note. But the note didn't mention his wife or his children as anyone would expect. Instead, it contained an apology to the FBI director and ended with this statement: "I guess now I will find out if there is a God."

I don't know what he did to feel so guilty. Was it some sort of treasonous act? I only know that he had judged himself as harshly as anyone can. He had determined that he was unworthy to go on living. He had condemned himself.

We humans are very good at condemnation, especially when it's our own sins that are in question. We've known people who have spent years punishing themselves. Some people won't allow themselves a moment's happiness because they feel they don't deserve it. The apostle Paul understood this aspect of our nature, which is why he took great care to address the condemnation issue. In his letter to the Romans, he wrote that "since we have been made right in God's sight by the blood of Christ, he will certainly save us from God's condemnation" (Romans 5:9).

It doesn't matter how much you think you deserve to be condemned.

It doesn't matter how badly you might *want* to be condemned.

It doesn't matter how harshly people might condemn you.

It doesn't even matter how determined you are to condemn yourself.

God won't condemn you if you are covered by the blood of Jesus.

We are a couple of guys who are always on the lookout for a good deal. Our eyes light up when we see a BOGO deal on ice cream at the supermarket. When someone offers us free tickets to a ballgame, you can count on us to take them. And yes, we always check the specials before we order in a restaurant. We are good deal experts. But we have never seen a good deal like the one God offers: no condemnation whatsoever in return for accepting Jesus as Lord and Savior.

But it occurs to us that not every reader of this book will know how to accept Jesus, so let us tell you.

You start with faith, which is believing that God is real and that he is who the Scriptures say he is. The Bible says that without faith it is impossible to please God (Hebrews 11:6).

Then comes what the Bible calls confession. It's simply acknowledging that you are a sinner in need of God's grace (1 John 1:9).

Next comes repentance. It's a decision you make to turn away from your sins and walk with God (2 Peter 3:9).

Finally, there's baptism. On the day the Church was born, people asked Peter what they needed to do to be saved. He said, "Each of you must turn from your sins and turn to God, and be baptized in the name of Jesus Christ for the forgiveness of your sins" (Acts 2:38).

These four steps are often called the Plan of Salvation. Some people believe you can become saved by uttering a simple prayer—often called the "sinner's prayer"—but we strongly disagree. The sinner's prayer is never practiced or taught in the Bible. Instead, when people are saved in the New Testament, we see them doing the four things we just listed: expressing faith, confessing sin, repenting, and being baptized.

If you haven't already, we encourage you to obey these commands from a sincere heart. There is no condemnation for anyone who does.

Life-Giving Fact #3: Friendship with God is restored when we are forgiven.

In Romans 5:10 there is a beautiful phrase that's easy to miss: "For since our friendship with God was restored." With all the other big ideas in this passage, it's easy to glide right over that one and not think about how incredible it is.

Have you ever been in a situation where a friendship you cherished was broken? Many years ago, I (Mark) discovered that an elder in the church I was serving had done something sinful that had deeply hurt one of our members. When I learned of this (from the person who was hurt) I had a decision to make. Would I expose his sinful action to the other elders or let it slide? Believe me, the temptation to let it slide was strong. I am not by nature a boat-rocker, and I knew that if I shined a light on his sin, our friendship would be over. Further, I knew he would see me as an enemy from that point on.

I chose to expose his sin.

In a specially called elder's meeting, I confronted the elder concerning his actions and had the wounded person on hand to verify the accusations. That meeting probably was the darkest two hours in all of my forty-six years of ministry.

The result was just as I expected. Our friendship was done. The man drew a bullseye on my chest and from that day forward did everything he could to make me look bad.

Now, jump forward ten years.

I had long since forgiven the man, moved to another church, and was living a nice life. I was at a Christian convention, in a large crowd of people, and suddenly heard my name being called. When I turned around, there was the man whose sin I had exposed years earlier, whom I believed probably still hated me. To my utter surprise, he approached me with a smile and stuck out his hand. I shook it as he said, "How have you been?" I answered, we exchanged pleasantries, and went our separate ways.

Clearly, he had buried the hatchet. I was glad. But the sick feeling that swirled in my stomach told me that while we would now be friendly to each other if our paths crossed, never, ever would we be friends.

Broken friendships are almost never restored. Hatchets can be buried, hands can be shaken, smiles can be offered, but 999 out of every 1,000 broken friendships never get back to the level of their former glory.

Not so with God.

Even after you've sinned egregiously and trampled on his will, he welcomes you back with open arms and treats you as if nothing happened. How is this possible? It's possible because he doesn't just forgive our sins, he forgets them. If that sounds too good to be true, consider God's own words: "I will forgive their wickedness, and I will never again remember their sins" (Hebrews 8:12).

This is one of the biggest factors in you being able to live guilt-free despite having a long RAP sheet. The fact that God doesn't even remember your sin means that you can let it go too. Isn't this the biggest reason why we have a hard time releasing our past mistakes, because we think all the people around us are remembering them every time they look at us? We feel self-conscious and unworthy. We imagine the negative thoughts that are going through their heads. But what if your sins were really and truly gone forever, and God doesn't even remember them?

We think it's impossible to overestimate the significance of this truth. How powerful it is to realize that when God forgives you, no record of your sin remains anywhere, and you are free to enjoy a beautiful, healthy friendship with God once again.

Life-Giving Fact #4: Rejoicing is the fruit of forgiveness.

"So now we can rejoice in our wonderful new relationship with God because our Lord Jesus Christ has made us friends of God" (Romans 5:11). We want to point out a couple of things in this verse. First, Paul calls our relationship with God new. This supports what we just said, that once we are forgiven our sin no longer exists. It's not being stored in a holding area somewhere. It's not in a file drawer or on some celestial hard drive waiting to be called up at the touch of a computer key. Rather, it's gone. Completely and permanently, which means our relationship with God is new again. There's no lingering odor to remind us of what we did and no nagging fear that it might come back to haunt us in the future.

Second, this wonderful new forgiveness-based relationship with God is called friendship. There are many kinds of relationships, but it seems to us that friendship is the highest and the best. Even married people who are very much in love will often say, "She's (or he's) my best friend," as if that's the thing that means the most to them. A son or daughter will often say, "My mom is my best friend," or "My dad is my best friend." You can get along just fine with people you live with, work with, go to school or church with, but it's not until you become true friends that the relationship goes to the next level and becomes special. There are reasons for this:

True friendship involves knowledge. That is, real friends know each other—the good and the bad—and accept each other, warts and all.

True friendship involves understanding. Knowing all about someone doesn't necessarily mean you understand them. We could both name people we've known for decades, yet still don't understand why they do the things they do. On the flipside, true friends will often say of each other, "He gets me," or "She gets me."

True friendship involves loyalty. You've heard the saying, "In times of trouble you find out who your friends are." It's just another way of saying that true friends can be counted on in good times and bad.

And finally, true friendship brings joy. I (Joe) rendezvous for a few days every year with a group of preachers I went to college with. It doesn't matter what kind of difficulties we might be dealing with in our separate churches, for a few days it all melts away like snowballs in the sun, and we just have a great time. I would say that the human relationship that brings about the most laughter and good times is friendship. Marriages often face great pressures. Parent-child relationships are notoriously difficult. Working relationships can be very stressful at times. But friendships are mostly fun and happy.

To wrap up this chapter, we want to show you a couple of verses from Habakkuk, that book in the Bible you can never find without checking the table of contents. Habakkuk wrote:

> Even though the fig trees have no blossoms, and there are no grapes on the vines; even though the olive crop fails, and the fields lie empty and barren; even though the flocks die in the fields, and the cattle barns are empty, yet I will rejoice in the LORD! I will be joyful in the God of my salvation! (Habakkuk 3:17-18)

If you have a long RAP sheet, you probably feel as much joy as a farmer looking out at his withered crops and dead livestock. Even though you know intellectually that God has forgiven you, you may feel no inclination to rejoice. That's when you must understand what Habakkuk is saying. Rejoicing is a choice you make not a gift that's dropped in your lap.

We love how author and physician Mike Mason says it: "I haven't the slightest doubt that God is bending over backward all day long to give me joy—but I must take it. Jesus stands at the crossroad pointing the way to joy, inviting and encouraging, but I must choose. Lasting happiness comes only through choice, through the making of countless small decisions, one day at a time. Once I see this, it's not hard to choose. The hard part is admitting I have a choice."[15]

You *do* have a choice!

Even if you've messed up big time. Even if the holier-than-thou crowd is using you for target practice.

---

[15] Mike Mason, *Champagne for the Soul* (Colorado Springs: Waterbrook, 2003), 52.

Even if you feel like an idiot every time you think about your RAP sheet, there's nothing to stop you from pushing all that aside and claiming Paul's beautiful words in Romans 5 as your very own:

God is not put off by your sin.

God's grace saves you from condemnation.

Friendship with God is restored when you are forgiven.

Rejoicing is the fruit of forgiveness.

No one can stop you from wallowing in your guilt if you're determined to do it, but why on earth would you? The whole message of the Bible is that God has done everything there is to do to make it possible for you to live guilt-free. Yes, even with a long RAP sheet.

8

YES, YOU *CAN* FIND THE "PERFECT" CHURCH

Church attendance is as vital to a disciple as a transfusion of rich, healthy blood to a sick man.
Dwight L. Moody

IN 2020, A SURVEY result was released by the Gallup organization that largely went unnoticed because we were all mentally and emotionally invested in the COVID-19 pandemic. Gallup said that for the first time ever the number of American adults who claimed no affiliation with a church, synagogue, or mosque dropped below 50 percent. The actual number was 47 percent, which was a 20 percent drop from the year 2000.[16]

You can see it in the number of churches we're losing. According to Lifeway Research, about 3,000 new churches were started in 2019, but approximately

---

[16] Jeffrey M. Jones, «U.S. Church Membership Falls Below Majority for First Time,» «Gallup, March 29, 2021, https://news.gallup.com/poll/341963/church-membership-falls-below-majority-first-time.aspx.

4,500 closed.[17] We're not mathematicians, but we're pretty sure that amounts to a sizeable hole in the bucket.

But this chapter is not about why churches are closing. Oh, yes, we'd love to sink our teeth into that subject, but we'll leave it for another time and focus instead on the issue that fits our theme: that growing number of people across the country who are now "former" church attenders. The number has never been bigger and appears to be growing year by year.

Based on our experience, these people are not wild-eyed malcontents who storm out the church doors screaming their complaints and shaking their fists at God and the preacher. Sure, there are some of those. But our take after talking to a lot of these people is that, for the most part, this new wave of former church attenders is made up mostly of decent people who, for whatever reason, have lost interest. Simply put, they started attending church because they were looking for something and eventually quit because they didn't find it.

And no, we're not blaming the church. It's true that sometimes churches are inept and ineffective, but it's also true that sometimes people go to church looking for the wrong things. We'll let others sort that out. In this chapter, we're going to focus on a statement we hear over and over again from former church

---

[17] Aaron Earls, «Protestant Church Closures Outpace Openings in U.S., Lifeway Research, May 25, 2021, https://research.lifeway.com/2021/05/25/protestant-church-closures-outpace-openings-in-u-s/.

attenders—one we think really needs to be addressed: "I just can't find a church I like."

There it is again, that word *can't*. We hear it all the time:

> "Since we've moved, we just can't find a church we like."

> "We've tried four or five different churches, and they were all ho-hum."

> "We love God, but we just can't find a church that the whole family likes."

Or we meet that nice family that comes through the door for the first time looking sharp and seeming like they would be fantastic church members. They're cheerful and friendly and wholesome looking and they're all carrying Bibles. Big Bibles. And we think, "Thank you, Lord, for sending us such a great family." Then the dad says something like this: "We've been to just about every church in town, and we just can't find one we like." And our hearts sink. We know they won't be with us very long.

Sadly, many people who have convinced themselves that they can't find a good church will stop going altogether. We meet people all the time who have dropped out of church, and the majority give this as the reason. Yes, some say they have been hurt or mistreated, but most just say they can't find a church they like.

Does Going to Church Matter?

We have noticed that people who are no longer going to church are overwhelmingly of the opinion that going to church is not of critical importance. The question is, do they really feel that way, or is it just a rationalization or a defense mechanism to be used when someone wants to talk to them about church? We'll not pass judgment on anybody, but we absolutely will tell you what our eighty-two combined years in the ministry have taught us.

Going to church matters to God.

The Church was God's idea, not man's. It's a community he established and ordained to provide care and nurturing, both physical and spiritual, for his people. Further, it's the way he chose to mobilize his people to impact the world with the Good News. Just think about all the good that has been done in the world by the Church: the souls that have been saved and the hospitals, orphanages, schools, homeless shelters, medical clinics, and crisis pregnancy centers that have been established around the world. Billions of people have been profoundly impacted for Christ by the Church. Heaven will largely be populated by people who found Jesus through the ministry of a local church. So pardon us if we have a hard time believing God would ever want to hear the words *church* and *doesn't matter* in the same sentence. On the contrary, we believe God would say to all of his people, "Get yourselves to church!"

In fact, he did say it through the writer of Hebrews: "And let us not neglect our meeting together, as some people do, but encourage one another, especially now that the day of his return is drawing near" (Hebrews 10:25).

We've heard people say, "My bass boat is my church. I can worship God on a quiet lake just as well as I can sitting in a church pew." We're well aware that Jesus used a fishing boat as a pulpit and that the disciples worshiped in a fishing boat. We're actually big fans of fishing boats. But we do not recommend standing before God someday trying to explain why you blew off the Church his only begotten Son suffered and died for in favor of some fiberglass, an outboard motor, and a plastic worm.

Going to church matters to your faith.

This is an easy one. We'll just say it straight out: We have never seen a person grow and get stronger in his or her faith after dropping out of church. That's over eight decades of ministry experience talking. We've seen enough people drop out of church to populate a small town. But never have we seen even one of them grow spiritually stronger. You know what usually happens if they don't quickly find a new church and get connected? They start sinking spiritually. It's not unusual for us to encounter them six months or a year later and discover that they're floundering. A happenstance conversation at the supermarket or the gas pump reveals that things aren't going well. We try to say something encouraging and let them know that the door is always open for them to come back to church—and sometimes they do. But more often they continue marching down the road that's taking them places they don't even want to go while continuing to argue that they don't need the Church.

Going to church matters to your family.

I (Joe) knew a kid named Chris. He grew up in a church where I was the youth minister. He was a terrific kid, but at sixteen, he was a little overdue for being baptized. He had learned everything he needed to know, and I had no doubt that he was a solid believer in Jesus. I and others had certainly encouraged him to be baptized, but for whatever reason he just hadn't yet made the decision.

And then one day he did.

I was actually baptizing someone else when he showed up and asked if he could be baptized too. It was a joy to lay him under the water and see the smile on his face when he came up.

That very night, Chris was in an auto accident that left him in a coma from which he never woke up. He was unconscious for two years before he finally went home to be with Jesus. Those two years were difficult beyond words for his parents, as you can imagine. But I will tell you this: The one thing that gave them peace was the fact that they had raised their son in church where he had found and accepted Jesus as his Savior. If you could ask them right now if going to church matters, they would have plenty to say.

Going to church matters to the lost.

I (Mark) baptized a man many years ago. The following week, we received the following letter from him in the church mail:

To my new church family:

Thank you for shining a light in the darkness that was strong and clear enough to guide me home. To everyone who gave an hour of service or a single dollar to keep the light shining, I am grateful. Most of all, thank you for loving me instead of judging me, for saving me a seat at the table even when I refused to believe there was a meal being served. The things you have done may seem small and inconsequential to you, but they changed everything for me.

No one understands how much fresh water matters like a man dying of thirst who is given a drink. And no one understands how much a church matters like a lost man who is saved because of its ministry. But churches are not buildings; they're people. They're men, women, children, and families that show up and give and serve so that the light will continue to shine. Without those faithful church-attenders, the light goes out.

In our view, it's high time we called the narrative that church attendance doesn't matter what it is: utter foolishness.

But that can't be the end of the discussion.

Leaving Your Church

Did you ever go out with someone you had a huge crush on only to be disappointed as you got better acquainted? Or maybe you were in love with someone for a time—perhaps years—but gradually the person changed, and your love started to wither. Such things can happen between churches as well as people. One of the reasons there are so many former church attenders is because so many people grow disenchanted and drop out. Our conversations with such people indicate that most people who drop out are not angry at God or down on the Church in general. They're just frustrated with the particular congregation they were attending.

There are two issues that need to be addressed here. One is leaving your church. The other is choosing a new one. We'll tackle the leaving issue first. And we hope you have your big boy/big girl pants on because we're not going to pull any punches.

The fact is some of the reasons people give for leaving their church make us want to bang our heads against a wall. We usually settle for rolling our eyes because the pain quotient is less and drywall repairs can be expensive, but really and truly, some of the reasons we hear add new meaning to the word *nonsense*. Here are our top three goofy reasons:

"I'm not being fed."

This might be the most common reason people give for leaving a church. It's a favorite because it makes the person who's leaving out to be a victim and places blame on the church. But we have a question. If you're forty years old and smart and healthy and you have to depend on someone else to feed you, are you a victim or a big baby who needs to grow up and take some responsibility?

Here's another question. Wouldn't you think that people who are concerned about being fed would hang out around the food? Yet many people who say this are Sunday-morning-only people who don't attend Bible studies or belong to a small group. Even when the spiritual food they claim to be hungry for is being served, they are nowhere to be seen.

Yes, we understand that some churches are weak when it comes to preaching and teaching. Sometimes shamefully weak. We get it. But even then, this reason doesn't sit well. It seems to say, "I came here to be served. I am my number one priority." That attitude is about as unchristian as you can get.

"I've been mistreated."

We'll just cut to the chase on this one. If mistreatment is the line in the sand you set for quitting something, you'll eventually quit everything: your school, your church, your job, and even your marriage. We find it ironic that people will complain all day long about their jobs and how mistreated and underpaid they are, yet they still show up every day like clockwork. But someone at church shows them a lack of consideration, and they storm out the door in a huff.

"All they talk about is money."

Again, the inconsistency here is breathtaking. The same people who gripe about the church being money hungry wouldn't think of boycotting their favorite restaurant that charges twenty bucks for a hamburger, fries, and a Coke. They happily cruise through their favorite coffee haunt and pay a ridiculous price for a few sips of caffeine. They spend hundreds of dollars to go to a football game that they could watch on TV for free. These people literally dole out fistfuls of cash right and left to secular entities that only have one goal: making money. But if the church asks for money to plant a church or help an orphanage, it is immediately labeled money hungry.

Suffice it to say, the reasons some people give for leaving a church are embarrassingly weak. That does not mean, however, that there aren't good reasons for leaving a church. Here are some that we would gladly endorse:

The Word of God has been abandoned and cultural trends have been embraced.

There sure is a lot of this going around. In an effort to be inclusive, many churches are backing away from the Bible's clear teachings regarding homosexuality, same-sex marriage, and transgender issues. On our travels we've noticed that many churches are now flying Pride flags on their buildings. And numerous high-profile preachers and influencers have dramatically changed, in some cases completely abandoning, the biblical truths they taught with passion just a few years ago. Our view is that if this happens in your church, you absolutely should leave.

Hurts have become overwhelming.

A number of years ago, I (Mark) advised a young woman and her husband to leave our church and go worship and serve somewhere else. The husband had cheated with another woman who was also a member of our church. The illicit relationship was over and both parties had repented, but the pain was very raw. Every time the man's wife encountered the other woman, she had flashbacks and panic attacks. If she even thought that her husband and the other woman had made eye contact, she became emotional. I met with them and counseled them to get away from the situation, at least for a while, so healing could take place. They did leave us and go to another church, and I'm happy to report that healing did come.

Bad things do sometimes happen in churches. We can forgive, but we are not robots. What we know in our heads sometimes takes a while to reach our hearts. There is no switch we can flip to make everything suddenly okay. Sometimes getting away (at least for a while) is the best medicine.

You're needed elsewhere to help the cause of Christ.

Let's say a struggling congregation within a reasonable driving distance from your house needs help. Or perhaps the church you attend has plans to plant a new congregation within a reasonable distance from where you live. In either case, leaving your church to assist the effort would be admirable.

Accessibility has become a problem.

When we were young, churches rarely relocated. Now, it's fairly common. Both of us oversaw relocations during our years of ministry. This means that a churchgoer who lives one mile from his or her church can wake up one morning and suddenly be living ten miles away. That might not sound like much, but in a metro area even a few miles can create logistical problems. When I (Mark) moved to Poinciana, Florida, in 1989, the population was four thousand. When I retired thirty-one years later, the population was eighty thousand, and rush hour traffic was a beast with fangs and claws. It could easily take fifty minutes to go ten miles. We had people, especially elderly people, who didn't feel comfortable driving in such crazy traffic. In every case, I applauded their decision to go to a church that was more accessible for them.

When Jesus and soul-saving cease to be priorities.
Jesus came to seek and save the lost and commanded his followers to go into all the world and make disciples. Many factors can affect a church's ability to evangelize, but there should at least be an effort made. Increasingly, churches are choosing to fight social justice battles instead of just telling people about Jesus. They are obsessed with staging protests, getting laws changed, and supporting (or defeating) political candidates, while Jesus gets lost in the shuffle. Our view is that Jesus—and *only* Jesus—is the answer for what ails this world. We would find it impossible to worship long term in a church that failed to unequivocally embrace this truth and let it shape its priorities.

The bottom line is, there are both good and bad reasons for leaving a church. We would encourage you to think and pray before you make such a decision. Talk to someone who is mature in the faith and will tell you the truth. Ask him or her if your reasons are petty or legitimate. Then pray some more.

If you do feel God is leading you to make a change, be careful how you leave.

Even if you have the very best of reasons for leaving your church, you can still make a mess of things if you're not careful. There are two mistakes you need to avoid. One is going out in a blaze of glory. You've got all kinds of frustrations bottled up, and you're determined to get them off your chest as you waltz out the door. The other is simply vanishing without a trace.

You don't say a word to anybody; you just disappear into thin air.

Neither of these choices is wise, or even kind. Airing out your pet peeves is pointless since you're not going to be attending there anymore anyway. It will only hurt people's feelings and build up resentment toward you. If there truly are issues giving you heartburn, the time to let them be known is long *before* you decide to leave, so maybe something can be done about them. And vanishing into thin air is no good either. People will wonder where you went and why. And yes, they will speculate, which always leads to erroneous conclusions, most of which will make you look bad because people tend to assume the worst.

The way to avoid all of this is simply to talk to one of your church leaders—probably the pastor—and explain what you're doing and why. You might be reluctant to do this because you think your pastor will try to talk you into staying but don't count on it. Most preachers are like the two of us: happy for people who are no longer supportive of our ministry to leave. It doesn't mean we're mad at them or no longer like them. We just know that it's hard enough to build a church when everyone is on board; it becomes even harder when you have people in the camp who are *not* on board.

Choosing a Church

Sadly, a hefty percentage of people who leave one church never find another; they just quit going. They might say they're going to find a new church. They might truly intend to. They might even look around a little. But if there's no obvious choice, they quickly discover that finding the right church can take a while and involve some effort. That's when they lose their heart for the task and put it on the back burner. Soon, when they're asked if they're going to church, out comes the answer we hate: "I just can't find a church I like."

We want to close out this book by giving you our six-point plan for finding not the perfect church but the perfect church *for you*. Yes, it's out there somewhere. Here are our suggestions:

Suggestion #1: Consider how the Bible is viewed.

If it is seen as anything other than the inerrant word of God, keep looking.

But here we have a word of caution. Don't just believe what the pastor or other members tell you. Many preachers who take a liberal view of Scripture are not upfront about it. They claim to believe the Bible is God's word because they know that's what some people want to hear, and they don't want to alienate anyone. But if pressed, they will say things like, "Our goal is to take God's inspired wisdom and fit it into a modern context." Or they may say that, yes, God inspired the Bible writers, but that the people who wrote it down were living in a very different time. Or they may say that *some* of the Bible is inspired, but parts of it are just the writers' opinions and not to be taken literally. Anytime the word *but* is spoken after the words *the Bible is the inspired, inerrant word of God* that's a huge red flag.

The best thing you can do is listen carefully to the sermons and judge for yourself. Are they expository or topical? That is, do they come right out of the biblical text, or do they sound like a motivational speech you might hear at a multi-level marketing rally? Are your toes ever stepped on? Are you ever challenged to make an uncomfortable change to your thinking or your lifestyle? You should be if the inspired word of God is really being preached. Hebrews says the Bible is sharper than any two-edge sword, cutting between soul and spirit and reaching our inner most desires (Hebrews 4:12). That can be very uncomfortable. Obviously, the word of God is also encouraging, inspiring, and comforting. But if you're going to a church where you're never made to feel uncomfortable, where the preaching always feels like a fluffy pillow, but never a razor-sharp sword, you probably need to move on.

Suggestion #2: Make missions a priority.

Does the church take the Great Commission seriously? Is it actively reaching out to the community, the surrounding area, and the world with the gospel? Not just with humanitarian support, but with the gospel? We are all in favor of helping to meet people's physical needs. The Church should be helping, of course. But we must remember that while there are many organizations helping with that effort, there is only one sharing the gospel, and that is the Church. If the Church fails, there is no safety net.

A commitment to the Great Commission—to going into all the world to preach and make disciples (Matthew 28:16-20)—is one of the primary characteristics of a great church. Why? Because it's hard. Far too many churches are content with their padded pews, their pablum sermons, the AC set on seventy-two degrees, and their once-a-month potluck. Missions-minded churches care more, go more, give more, pray more, and ultimately baptize more.

If you come to Tomoka Christian, you'll hear me (Joe) making some kind of Great Commission-related plea every single Sunday. I might parade a mission team that's heading off to some third-world country across the stage and ask the people to pray for them. I might report on the progress of a new church we recently planted in Egypt. I might ask for a special offering to support an urgent need that one of our missionaries has. My point is this: if you get involved in a missions-minded church, more will be asked of you, but you can know for sure that you're helping to make a real difference for Christ. If, on the other hand, the monthly church potluck is your congregation's premier act of sharing, not so much.

Suggestion #3: Don't be wooed by externals.

Here's a disheartening moment that both of us have experienced many times:

A good family relocates to another town (or even another state) and can no longer attend our church. We hate to lose them but fully understand. It happens in a society as mobile as ours.

A year later the family comes back for a visit. We're thrilled to see them and hugs are given all around. Naturally, we ask, "Have you found a good church?" And the answer comes back: "Oh, yes, we love our new church. They have a gorgeous building and a band you wouldn't believe. They also have a gymnasium, so the boys have gotten involved in basketball. And the two of us are playing in the Thursday night coed softball league."

We say, "Oh really? What church is it?"

And then our hearts sink when they name a church or denomination that has a notorious reputation for watering down the gospel, for being more concerned about accommodating cultural trends than preaching God's truth.

We're not against beautiful buildings or fantastic worship bands or sports. We just think it's tragic when those "shiny objects" so captivate people that they don't stop to consider the more important things.

Canceling Can't

When I (Mark) was young, a church about one hundred miles from where I lived was looking for a preacher and contacted me, curious to know if I'd be interested in interviewing for the position. I knew about the church. It was in an upscale area and had a beautiful building, much bigger and nicer than the church I was currently serving. I told them that I would be honored to sit for an interview and immediately kicked on the afterburners to put my prayer life in warp speed. I wanted that job!

I didn't get it.

They didn't even call me to come for an interview after asking if I would be interested. It almost felt like an April Fool's joke.

But here's the reason I'm telling you this story.

Less than one year after that church contacted me about a possible interview, news broke that the church had been exposed as being massively corrupt. Multiple scandals were reported in the news, people were fired, charges were pressed, and people left the church in droves.

I believe God spared me from being right in the middle of that—and taught me a valuable lesson about being wooed by externals.

Somehow, we know that looks aren't everything. Remember *Gilligan's Island*, the sixties sit-com about tourists stranded or a deserted island? Ginger was the jaw-dropping, ravishing beauty. Mary Ann was the cute-as-a-button girl next door. Did you know that Mary Ann got twice as many fan letters as Ginger?

And when CBS ran surveys to see what character was most popular, Mary Ann usually won by a margin of three to one?[18]

Yes, we know that looks aren't everything, but sometimes we forget when looking for a church.

Suggestion #4: Consider opportunities for service.

You're not going there to be a consumer; you're going to give your worship, your money, and your service.

I (Joe) have even gone so far as to stop using the word *membership*. Rather than speaking about our good Tomoka people as being church members, I refer to them as church partners. To me, membership is about what I can get. If I am a member of Sam's Club, I get the privilege of shopping there and a good price on a package of one hundred rolls of toilet paper that I can barely squeeze into my oversized shopping cart. If I am a member of the country club, I get reduced greens fees and a discount in the pro shop. Membership has its privileges.

Partnership, on the other hand, is about what I can give. When I talk to people who are interested in Tomoka Christian Church, I tell them straight up that we're looking for people who want to partner with us in winning souls for Jesus. We're not just looking for people to fill seats on Sunday morning. Our goal is not

---

[18] Phil Luciano, "Ginger or Mary Ann? The Professor knew the answer," *Journal Star*, December 30, 2020, https://www.pjstar.com/story/news/columns/luciano/2020/12/30/luciano-ginger-mary-ann-professor-knew-answer/4093097001/#.

to build an audience, it's to build an army. If people want to be spectators, they should go to the movies or to a ballgame. If they come to Tomoka, they should be ready to get involved.

Your attitude in this area will determine how much your church means to you. If it's just a show you go to once a week, it will mean very little. Shows are a dime a dozen: plays, concerts, TV shows, movies, sporting events, and even podcasts. You can watch a million shows without leaving your recliner. With livestreaming now being so common, you can even watch church from the comfort of your recliner while munching popcorn.

In order for your church to mean anything to you, you must get involved. So look for a church that is active, that offers opportunities for you to use your talents and make a difference for Jesus. Get out of your recliner and go.

Suggestion #5: Think about what the church offers your family.

You have only a few years with your children. Then they're going to go out into a world that is almost completely antagonistic toward true, biblical Christianity. If you're looking for a church, it would make no sense to disregard their spiritual needs. For example, a church with no ministry to teens would not be a great choice if you have two or three teenagers. The preacher might counter by saying, "But you could come here and help us *start* a ministry to teens." And that might be true. Don't discount the possibility. On the other hand, if the church has been around for many years and still doesn't have a ministry to teens, there's probably a deeper reason.

Back when Tomoka was a struggling little church of 125, I (Joe) actually told some moms and dads who were looking for a church that their kids would be better off at a congregation nearby. I even offered to help them get connected there. I know some people—especially preachers—will read this and say I'm crazy, but we just weren't ready to give those families what they needed, and I knew it.

I always tried to put myself in the place of the family that was searching for a church and to treat them the way I would want to be treated. I wouldn't want a preacher to try to woo me into his church to fill a few more seats if he knew his church wasn't capable of ministering to my family. I would want him to be honest with me and tell me if there was a better option somewhere nearby. And yes, I believe God honors that kind of "people first" attitude. Because we were honest with people and did what we thought was best for them, God kept sending more people to us. Today, Tomoka Christian runs in the thousands.

Suggestion #6: Avoid any church that has a history of trouble.

I (Mark) once visited a congregation that had three hundred people in their auditorium for their Sunday morning service. The problem was that their auditorium seated five thousand. Do the math on that. For every seat filled, there were well over one hundred empty seats! And no, they didn't build too much building. They actually filled the building at one time, but a years-long series of scandals and church fights had reduced the body almost to nothing.

That's an extreme example, but there's an important reminder in it: some churches are unhealthy to the point of being toxic. You might not be able to sense it as easily as I could in the example mentioned above because churches always try to put their best foot forward for new people. They might even exaggerate a little to make themselves look better than they really are. That's why it's important to ask questions about the church's history, such as:

> Has there ever been a church split? If so, how long ago did it happen and what caused it?

> What is the church's attendance trajectory? Is it generally upward, or is it decreasing? And if it is decreasing, is it gradually decreasing or plummeting? And what reasons are the for this decrease?

How often does the church get a new preacher? How many preachers has the church had in the last twenty years?

Has there ever been a financial scandal? Are the books open for inspection, or is everything handled secretly?

Let me be quick to say that *every* church has *some* trouble. Just because a church has had some problems doesn't mean it isn't a great church. Sometimes broken churches get fixed and go on to do great things. My point is simply that you should do a little research and find out.

The title of this chapter is, "Yes, You Can Find the 'Perfect' Church." No, we don't believe there's a "perfect" church out there. But we do believe there's a perfect church *for you*. Perfect in the sense that it preaches and teaches the whole counsel of God without apology. Perfect in the sense that it cares deeply about the lost. Perfect in the sense that it's well positioned to help you grow in Christ. Perfect in the sense that it will give you opportunities to give and serve. Sure, it may get a little messy sometimes, just like work or school or even family life gets a little messy. *People* are messy! But messy is not the same as broken or dysfunctional or toxic. Those are the things you need to be wary of.

At the end of the day, all of the excuses you come up with to miss church or drop out of church or give up looking for a good church—*all* of them—come from the pit of hell. Isolating you from the body of Christ is a brilliant tactical move on Satan's part. Divide and conquer is the oldest—and the most effective—war strategy in existence. Don't fall for it. There *is* a church that's perfect for you. Find it and go.

Questions for Quiet Reflection or Group Discussion

From Mark and Joe:

Please remember to be thoughtful when answering discussion questions in a group setting. While it's great to be authentic, some of your thoughts, past experiences, or personal information may be best kept private. It is our intent with these questions to help you reflect on the content of this book. In no way do we want to put you in an awkward situation where you feel pressured to reveal too much. Always err on the side of caution. And remember, you can always talk to God when everyone else has gone home.

Chapter 1
YES, YOU *CAN* GET OUT OF THAT PIT

1. If you're currently in a pit (a bad, seemingly hopeless situation), is it of the natural, man-made variety, or did you dig it yourself? If you dug it yourself, what is one choice you made that, more than anything else, created the problem?

2. How has your pit experience affected your relationship with God? With your family and friends? How has it affected your feelings toward yourself?

3. There's an old saying: "If you've dug yourself into a hole, stop digging." If your pit is the result of your own actions, have you stopped digging? If not, why?

4. One of the main "climbing tools" you have at your disposal is repentance. Even if you have stopped digging for the moment, have you truly repented of your sin? What specific changes in your life would indicate true repentance?

Chapter 2
YES, YOU *CAN* FIND JUSTICE IN AN UNJUST WORLD

1. What are some examples of injustice that bother you the most? Can you name a situation in your own life where you were a victim of injustice?

2. How do you react to God's sovereignty, the fact that he is the Master of creation and in charge of everything? Does it trouble you? Do you sometimes feel resentment toward him when you see injustice happening?

QUESTIONS FOR QUIET REFLECTION OR GROUP DISCUSSION

3. Joseph, who was treated unjustly numerous times, eventually found justice. Of the four qualities he demonstrated—righteousness, patience, humility, and trust—which one do you struggle with the most? What could you do to strengthen yourself in that area of weakness?

4. What is the ultimate hope every Christian has when it comes to injustice? (See 2 Corinthians 4:16–18) Are you certain of that hope for yourself? If not, who is someone you could talk to who could help you?

Chapter 3
YES, YOU *CAN* FEEL GOOD ABOUT YOUR FUTURE IN A DETERIORATING WORLD

1. Name some things that are currently happening in our world that trouble you. How often do you think about them? Do you worry enough to lose sleep or feel nervous? What do you do when strong feelings of anxiety come upon you? What *should* you do?

2. "Whether or not we walk with God doesn't depend on God; it depends on us." How faithfully have you walked with God? If you haven't been faithful, why not? What, specifically, could you do to improve in that area? How would walking more closely with God help your view of the future?

3. God has promised to work all things together for good for those who love him and are called by him (Romans 8:28). Can you give an example of how God brought good out of something bad that happened? How does God's ability to do this affect your outlook on life?

4. How much do you think about heaven? If you don't think about it much, why do you think you don't? What could you do to put heaven more on your mind?

Chapter 4
YES, YOU *CAN* LIVE COURAGEOUSLY IN A TERRIFYING WORLD

1. What are your greatest fears? Has fear shrunk your life? Are there things you don't do and places you don't go because of fear?

2. After boasting that he never would, Peter betrayed Jesus because he was afraid. Has fear ever caused you to make a bad spiritual decision? What did you learn from that experience?

3. On the day of Pentecost, Peter courageously condemned the Jews for murdering Jesus and challenged them to accept Jesus as Lord and Savior. Do you think he would have been so courageous if he hadn't had his fellow apostles standing at his

QUESTIONS FOR QUIET REFLECTION OR GROUP DISCUSSION

side? Do you have friends that give you courage? If not, do you need different friends?

4. Peter stepped over the side of a fishing boat into crashing waves because he was convinced Jesus could enable him to walk on water. How convinced are you of Jesus's power? What are some things you have done that demonstrate your faith in Jesus's power? What are some things you could do that would help your faith grow even stronger?

Chapter 5
YES, YOU *CAN* CONQUER YOUR BESETTING SIN

1. What is your besetting sin? (Please use discretion if you are in a group discussion.) What degree of trouble and pain has it brought you? How would your life change if you could overcome it? What efforts have you made?

2. After his affair with Bathsheba, David prayed that God would change his heart (Psalm 51:10). Have you ever prayed that prayer? If not, why? What steps could you take to better guard your heart (Proverbs 4:23)?

3. Pruning is an important step in overcoming stubborn sin. Can you name something unhealthy that you have pruned out of your life in the past? What

could you prune out of your life now that would reduce the hold your besetting sin has on you?

4. When an activity is pruned out of your life, a void is left that must be filled. What could you do that would fill that empty space with something positive?

Chapter 6
YES, YOU *CAN* LIVE RIGHTEOUSLY IN A CESSPOOL

1. How have the rapidly declining morals in America affected you and your family? Have you noticed yourself becoming more permissive as our culture sinks deeper into immorality? Do you find yourself doing and saying things that at one time would have been completely off-limits?

2. There are four strategies for living righteously mentioned in this chapter. They are self-discipline, separation, saturation, and seriousness. Which of these have you tried? How have they worked? Have you grown discouraged? What is your current strategy?

3. Surrender involves giving up your life for Jesus's sake. What do you think that involves? How is giving up your life to stay pure different from fighting to stay pure?

QUESTIONS FOR QUIET REFLECTION OR GROUP DISCUSSION

4. Surrender must be unconditional to work. Have you been guilty of trying to make deals with God? What do you need to give up to be fully surrendered?

Chapter 7
YES, YOU *CAN* LIVE GUILT-FREE WITH A LONG RAP SHEET

1. We've all sinned, but did you have a lifestyle of sin in your past? Is there someone who hates you because of what you did? Are some of your family relationships broken because of your actions? If so, in what ways have these facts affected your life?

2. What has been your feeling about God's grace as it relates to your sin? Have you worried that his grace might not cover your sin? If so, what has caused you to think this? How do the stories of people in the Bible who sinned greatly but were still forgiven by God influence your thinking?

3. Have you accepted Jesus Christ as your Lord and Savior? If so, have you followed through on that decision and been baptized? If not, why? If so, how have these choices changed the way you think or feel?

4. If you are forgiven, you are a friend of God. How does that thought make you feel? How does it affect your choices?

Chapter 8
YES, YOU *CAN* FIND THE "PERFECT" CHURCH

1. Are you currently attending a church regularly? If not, why? Is your lack of attendance because of a frustration related to the church itself? If so, explain.

2. If you have left a church recently, explain why you made that decision. Looking back, do you believe your decision was a good one? Were you perhaps a bit harsh or hasty in your decision? Since you left, have you found another church to attend? If not, why?

3. When you consider a church, how much are you influenced by externals (building, property, technology, etc.)? In your opinion, what are the two or three most important things a church can have going for it? What is one thing that immediately turns you off about a church?

4. React to this statement from Joe: "We're not just looking for people to fill seats on Sunday morning. Our goal is not to build an audience; it's to build

QUESTIONS FOR QUIET REFLECTION OR GROUP DISCUSSION

an army." In your church experience, are you more of a spectator or a partner? How do you believe this choice impacts your church experience?

About the Authors

MARK ATTEBERRY SPENT FORTY-SIX years in ministry, with the last thirty-one of those years at Poinciana Christian Church in Kissimmee, Florida. In 2003, Mark's first book, *The Samson Syndrome*, was published by Thomas Nelson Publishers. Since then, he has become an award-winning author with twenty-one books in his body of work. Since retiring from full-time ministry in 2020, Mark has continued to write and teach at Advance Center for Ministry Training, a college-level school for aspiring preachers. Recently, he's started preaching again at the First Christian Church of Frostproof, Florida.

On the personal side, Mark is married to Marilyn, his high school sweetheart. They have one daughter and two extraordinary grandchildren who are among the greatest the world has ever known.

You can visit Mark's website at markatteberry.net.

About the Authors

Joe Putting is a pulls-no-punches pastor, leader, and speaker who is fully committed to winning as many souls to Christ as possible. Under his leadership, Tomoka Christian Church has planted tens of thousands of churches all around the world, even in countries where Christianity is illegal. Highly educated with a bachelor's degree, three master's degrees, and a PhD, Joe nevertheless comes across as completely down to earth. He is the chairman of the board for Christian Arabic Services and serves on the board for Florida Church Planters. His book *We Said Yes!* is transforming the way churches do missions.

Joe has been married to his wife, Luanne, for thirty-nine years, and together they have five children. Joe has been the pastor at Tomoka Christian Church in Ormond Beach, Florida for thirty-two years.

You can visit Joe's website at Joe-Putting.com.

Mark and Joe would like to thank the team at Illumify Media for a fantastic publishing experience. Michael Klassen, Geoff Stone, Jen Clark, and Debbie Lewis are true professionals who made the journey fun and exciting.

www.ingramcontent.com/pod-product-compliance
Lightning Source LLC
Chambersburg PA
CBHW032225080426
42735CB00008B/718